Black Looks
& Black Acts

PETER LANG
New York • Washington, D.C./Baltimore • Bern
Frankfurt am Main • Berlin • Brussels • Vienna • Oxford

Ritashona Simpson

Black Looks
& Black Acts

The Language of Toni Morrison
in *The Bluest Eye* and *Beloved*

PETER LANG
New York • Washington, D.C./Baltimore • Bern
Frankfurt am Main • Berlin • Brussels • Vienna • Oxford

Library of Congress Cataloging-in-Publication Data

Simpson, Ritashona.
Black looks and Black acts: the language of Toni Morrison
in The bluest eye and Beloved / Ritashona Simpson.
p. cm.
Includes bibliographical references.
1. Morrison, Toni—Language. 2. Morrison, Toni. Bluest eye.
3. Morrison, Toni. Beloved. 4. African Americans—Languages.
5. African Americans—Race identity. 6. African Americans in literature.
7. Race in literature. I. Title.
PS3563.08749Z855   813'.54—dc22   2006101475
ISBN 978-0-8204-9530-9

Bibliographic information published by **Die Deutsche Bibliothek**.
Die Deutsche Bibliothek lists this publication in the "Deutsche
Nationalbibliografie"; detailed bibliographic data is available
on the Internet at http://dnb.ddb.de/.

Cover images by Yaalieth Simpson

Cover design by Sophie Boorsch Appel

The paper in this book meets the guidelines for permanence and durability
of the Committee on Production Guidelines for Book Longevity
of the Council of Library Resources.

© 2007 Peter Lang Publishing, Inc., New York
29 Broadway, 18th floor, New York, NY 10006
www.peterlang.com

Printed in Germany

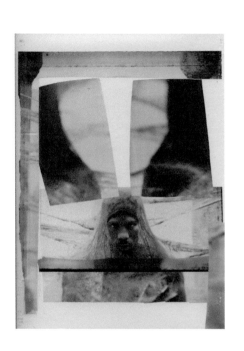

Dedication:

I dedicate my first book to the loving memory of Dr. John H. Simpson,
my father, my mentor, and my best friend:
Thanks be to God for His Unspeakable Gift.
(II Corinthians 9:15)

CONTENTS

ACKNOWLEDGMENTS

I would like to thank my sister, Dr. Yaalieth Simpson, visiting professor at Florida State University, for providing the art work for this book.

Professors Cheryl Wall, Fran Bartkowski, Carolyn Williams, and Marianne Dekoven all provided supportive and inciteful comments on this book when it was a dissertation. Professor Wall went above and beyond the call of duty when she encouraged me to publish my dissertation after I completed graduate school.

I thank my mother, Minister Wallie Simpson, for her prayers and for her guidance as my mentor and principal at the Harlem International Community School.

INTRODUCTION

Black Looks and Black Acts:
Toni Morrison's Black English

In her book, *Black Looks*, bell hooks raises important issues about race and representation:

> For those of us who dare to desire differently, who seek to look away from the conventional ways of seeing blackness and ourselves, the issue of race and representation is not just a question of critiquing the status quo. It is also about transforming the image, creating alternatives, asking ourselves questions about what types of images subvert, pose critical alternatives, and transform our worldviews and move us away from dualistic thinking about good and bad. (4)

Bell hooks explores the images associated with Blacks in the mass media. However, the issues she raises also apply to language. This dissertation focuses on Morrison's contribution to the transforming image of the language associated with Blacks and discusses the extent to which her transformation is "creative," "poses critical alternatives," and challenges "dualistic thinking" about racialized language.

Language has long been racialized in America. A plethora of studies generated in the late 1960's and early 1970's[1] determines that a set of nonstandard English features form a dialect most often recognized and spoken by Blacks.[2] J.L. Dillard's study on Black English was among the first to propose an idea that later garnered attention and currency among linguists: these linguistic features are somehow related to the first languages of the slaves brought from Africa.

Although linguists are able to document features of spoken Black English with a high degree of consistency, the written representation of Black English has, from its inception, been fairly inconsistent. Black English is a dialect which has no standard written form. For this reason, the language used to represent Blacks has changed in the American media over the centuries. Sylvia Holton and Walter Brasch document the changing image of the language used to represent Blacks. Both reach similar conclusions about its metamorphosis. Brasch notes the most striking changes over three hundred years (1650–1980):

> As the visibility of the Black increased, Black language in the mass media became more readable . . . It is probable that the early writers of Black English . . . were not aware of the subtle nuances of language. . . . They knew there were differences, but unsure about what those differences were, they inserted whatever happened to be handy . . . But as more and more writers became aware of Black English, whether they called it that or not, the recording of the language improved, for each writer was now able to draw upon the literary productivity of every other writer. (xviii)

Brasch's observations are evidenced in comparisons between earlier and later representations of Black English. Nineteenth century literature and drama were filled with comic and derogatory representations of Black language intended to suggest the common belief that Blacks were inferior.[3] The malapropisms, eye dialect (words spelled incorrectly to suggest their distinction as dialect and not to suggest sound or sense), orthography (spelling used to suggest sound), grammar and syntax, were calculated to impress the difference of Black language. One of the worst examples of this minstrel dialect is found in the work of Dan Emmett:

> I jis tole yoa now, dat de hegeniture ob my connuberalness substancherates its own casloozens . . . De quinin ob my 'scoas, dis ebenin, am tended to sessiate de sessity ob yoa own mine being kept cool. . . .[4]

No doubt, the carefully crafted Standard English of the slave narratives, written by the likes of Frederick Douglass, Harriet Jacobs, and Olaudah Equiano contradicted and challenged the blatant racist assumptions promoted by such works. By asserting their claims to literacy, these Blacks proved themselves to be beyond the boundaries of fixed associations of race and writing.

If the nineteenth century were marked by casual and insidiously cryptic forms of language portrayed in so many of the dialect poetry and tales[5] and plantation novels[6] issued during this time, the beginning of the twentieth century marked a century of the rebirth of Black English, as Black writers began to change its form and shape its image. During this time, as Holton[7] notes, the representation of Black English would:

> be indicated in writing more by grammatical than by phonological features. It would represent the language of black folk, the poor, whether country or city people . . . [it] was to become an identifying racial characteristic that later black writers would display with pride. (140)

Holton is careful to give a broad overview of the changes observed in material produced by writers during the twentieth century. Her study is important precisely because it focuses on the permeations of language produced by Black writers manifested not simply in its grammar and syntax and spelling but also in its rhythm and rhetoric. Likewise, several major studies of Black vernacular deserve attention: Henry Louis Gates, Houston Baker, and Karla Holloway,[8] Barbara Johnson, and Mae Henderson have all produced theories of the Black vernacular which reflect the impact of folk traditions and music upon the style of language used by Blacks.

Still, there is need for much more work to be done on the contributions Black writers have made collectively to the language used to represent Blacks. While smaller studies have been done on the representations of Black dialect in the work of major twentieth century Black writers, extensive research on this topic has yet to be published on the work of Toni Morrison,[9] even though her acquisition of the 1993 Nobel Prize in literature heralds the importance of her work.

It is my privilege to present in this dissertation a close analysis of Toni Morrison's contribution to the language used to represent race in two of her novels, *The Bluest Eye* and *Beloved.* It stems from my increased awareness of the construction of written Black language and curiosity about how a masterful writer such as Morrison constructs such language by giving leeway to her creative poetic intuition and to her discerning ear for the sound and sense of spoken Black language.

Like Zora Neale Hurston, Morrison has published her own observations about the form of Black English. Morrison's own critique of the first lines of each of her novels in her essay "Unspeakable Things Unspoken" is the best published scholarship of her work, which unequivocally calls for critics to pay attention to the craft of the language formation; her tantalizingly short and sharp statements on her attempts to produce a language "worthy of the race" beckons close critical attention to her theory of how she represents race in language, and the application of this theory to her work:

> my choices of language (speakerly, aural, colloquial), my reliance for full comprehension on codes embedded in black culture, my effort to effect immediate co-conspiracy and intimacy (without any distancing, explanatory fabric), as well as my (failed) attempt to shape a silence while breaking it are attempts (many unsatisfactory) to transfigure the complexity and wealth of Afro-American culture into a language worthy of the culture. (23)

The title of this dissertation, Black Looks and Black Acts, stems from my understanding of what Morrison, and in retrospect all Black writers, have done for the development of the language used to represent Blacks. Here, Morrison describes her attempts to expand the language to go beyond or reconstruct what I call its physiognomy, for lack of a better term. The emphasis for early writers of Black dialect was on its looks. The nonstandard grammar, syntax, and spelling of the early Black written English were contorted into strikingly nonsensical and comical utterances: the sense of difference was often forced upon the eye. In such a way racists promoted the idea of essential difference which could be easily identified: negative differences in language imputed negative differences to dark skin color. However, what the Black writers have done to such a representation involves a stunning reversal of the assumptions about racial difference in language. They have, as noted earlier, reduced the differences noticed immediately with the eye: the dialect is simplified and heavy phonological representations (and eye dialect) have disappeared. In its place, Black writers such as Morrison have increased what is not often immediately visible in the grammar, syntax, or spelling. Morrison focuses instead on allowing the written language to sound Black—to suggest through its arrangement the way she hears it orally—rather than to arrange its grammatical features to appear Black. Secondly, Morrison focuses on what cannot be explicitly related by "Black" features of language at all: the creation of a voice which is never heard or the revelation of the atmosphere associated with oral culture.

As I will argue in my dissertation, Morrison uses Standard English to achieve her goal of creating these effects. However, when she uses standard English for this purpose, the language is Black—not because it has the looks conventionally associated with Black race (nonstandard grammar)—but because it serves the goal she has defined for achieving a language worthy of the Black culture. Looks and acts are two sides of the same coin. Simply put, the looks include the physiognomy of the language and the acts include the ways in which the writer uses language in the service of representing race.

The terms Black **looks** and Black **acts** are used here as a frame, a vantage point, through which the variety of language used by Morrison can be examined. This vantage point reveals no more and no less than what Dexter Fisher and Robert Stepto witnessed two decades ago in the language written by Blacks:

> the oral tradition is not a formless sea in which myths, archetypes, narrative structures, and salient themes float. Nor is it an eddy in the mainstream of American language in which oddments of quaint expressions and colorful terms peculiar to the black speech community whirl about. That oral tradition is also a language with a grammar, a syntax, and standards of eloquence of its own . . . The Afro-American artist is just as bicultural, just as much an heir to legitimate linguistic traditions, in the area of language as he is in the area of literary forms: Black speech is to formal English as the oral tradition is to the literate tradition. (237)

Fisher and Stepto describe a wide range of literary traditions which Black writers may draw upon: what they call "black speech" is the "poetic diction" which mediates between the traditions named above (239). What I attempt to do in this dissertation is to show how Morrison mediates between these traditions and to place an emphasis on how such a mediation has made an impact on the "looks" of the language associated with Blacks in literature. In short, my dissertation shows the degree to which she uses grammar, syntax and spelling to make the language look Black. Paradoxically, Morrison also arranges the grammar, syntax, and spelling in ways that are unconventionally Black to transform the nature of Black looks: she uses Standard English to accomplish changes in voice, rhetoric, and narration for the purposes of making the language express the Black culture she describes.

There are four chapters. The first two chapters explore the issues described above in *The Bluest Eye* and the second two chapters explore these issues in *Beloved*. In Chapter 1, I examine the syntax, orthography, and grammatical patterns of the language used by the characters. I analyze the poetic function which nonstandard and standard dialect serve in this novel. In Chapter 2, I focus on how Morrison uses the written word to depict the realm of orality, that part of spoken language which cannot be captured on the page. She also uses the rhetorical and narrative structures of the book to develop the voices of those who do not break their silences. Chapter 3 continues to explore the development of such silences described in Chapter 2 in *Beloved*. The final Chapter returns to a close examination of the grammar, syntax, and spelling used to signify race in the character of Beloved.

I have chosen to analyze *The Bluest Eye* and *Beloved* because I have noticed that even though a span of almost two decades separates their publications, a continuity of language development can be traced between them. I will focus on the similarities in the language Morrison uses to represent Pecola and Beloved. More importantly, however, I trace Morrison's development of the language she uses to express the Black culture described in these works. Experiments in narrative, rhetoric, and dialect in *The Bluest Eye* are honed and polished in *Beloved*.

I draw upon a wide variety of tools to accomplish the goals of this dissertation. One methodological approach which distinguishes my work from other criticism of Morrison is my use of the research found in the study of linguistics. I rely heavily on the historiography of Black English to discern the patterns of Black speech used by Morrison. For instance, Chapter 4 discuses the historiography of Black English. Chapters 1 and 4 entail a close reading of the grammar of dialect as described by linguists. Chapter 2 especially relies on the work of linguists such as Deborah Tannen, M.M. Bakhtin, and V.N. Volosinov for discussions on the rhetoric of orality and voice. However, Chapter 3 places Morrison's contributions to language within the larger context of Black literary history. In each chapter, I observe how the analysis of linguistic aspects of Morrison's work enhances my understanding of her work as literature.

ELEMENTS OF FEELING, SILENCE, AND SOUND: THE GRAMMAR OF BLACK AND STANDARD ENGLISH IN *THE BLUEST EYE*

Several questions are raised by the variety of dialect found in Toni Morrison's *The Bluest Eye*. Why is it that the language of some of the characters, such as Pauline and Aunt Jimmy, contains more features of Black dialect[1] than some of the other Black characters such as Maureen or Soaphead? Why do some of the White characters, the hunters for example, speak Black English? Why does Pecola speak Standard English when she is insane and Black English when she is "normal"? Why is it that the protagonist, Pecola, imagines that her Black English-speaking parents use Standard English?

My explanation for why these and other lines of development occur in the *Bluest Eye* yields a paradox. On the one hand, Morrison's language strives to approximate reality. As a result, her de-emphasis on pronunciation and grammatical features of Black dialect accurately reflects a bi-dialectal reality observed by linguists such as John Baugh, Geneva Smitherman, Ralph Fasold, and Roger Shuy. These linguists have observed that speakers of Black English sometimes use Standard English and sometimes use a modified form of Black English. There is a variety of speech styles and a number of speakers who use more than one style. In other words, her characters' use of a mixture of both standard and Black English reflects the way the Black community speaks.[2]

On the other hand, Morrison's grammatical choices in this novel are also governed by the poetic realm. Like masks, these features of standard and Black dialect are infused with meaning and acquire symbolic value. Thus, Black and standard dialects appear together in ordinary and extraordinary linguistic events shaped by a creative and performative impulse at the very moment when they are also determined by a realistic and pragmatic impulse. In these events, the poetic realm dictates a reduction of Black English where you least expect it. In other words, the novel strives to represent accurately the speech of its characters based on their race, and its linguistic choices are also shaped by literary requirements.

In this chapter, I evaluate samples of speech from each of the main characters and analyze patterns of Black and standard dialect. I have grouped these samples within several categories, but the boundaries of these categories remain fluid and indeterminate. Each category contains samples of Black and/or Standard English with varying degrees of consistency; each category sounds a particular chord of poetic expression.

In the first group, the characters speak predominantly Black English; however, the speech contains a few instances where Black and Standard English are used interchangeably. The narrator's working class mother, Mrs. MacTeer, is one example from this category. In the following passage, Mrs. MacTeer, or Mama, as the narrator calls her, chastises the protagonist, little Pecola, a visitor in her house who has helped herself to three quarts of milk. I have underlined the words I wish to emphasize. The italics are Morrison's.

> I don't know what I'm *suppose* to be running here, a charity ward,
> I guess . . . I ain't *supposed* to have *nothing*. I'm *supposed* to end up
> In the poorhouse . . . Folks just spend all *their* time trying to figure out
> Ways to send *me* to the poorhouse. I got *about* as much business
> With another mouth to feed as a cat with side pockets . . . Bible
> *say* watch as *well* as pray. Folks just dump *they* children off on you
> And go on 'bout *they* business . . . That thought *don't* cross *they* mind. (23)

A brief analysis of the passage above demonstrates two things. First, there is a plethora of grammatical and orthographical features of Black English. Secondly, the grammar is realistic in the sense that the Black English here conforms to the rules of spoken Black English observed by linguists. To give a few examples to demonstrate what I mean: the sentence, "I ain't supposed to have nothing," contains an example of "multiple negation." Black English can use more than two or three negatives in a given sentence: but multiple negation simply indicates one negative in the sentence, not several (Burling, 56). Thus the sentence actually means "I am not supposed to have anything." "Ain't," is the Black English equivalent of "am not," in this sentence (Burling, 70). There is also a lack of subject-verb agreement in this passage. In the phrase, "Bible say," the third person plural of the verb 'say' replaces the standard third person singular (Burling, 49). Finally, in the phrase, "that thought don't cross," 'don't' is the Black English term which replaces the standard 'does not' (Fasold, 63).

In the midst of this Black English lies a surprising appearance of Standard English. Mama uses "suppose" and "supposed" interchangeably. When the verb "suppose" loses its -ed ending during the time it is pronounced, the orthography reflects a rule for pronunciation in Black English. In this rule, speakers do not pronounce the "d" at the end of a word (Burling, 51). Although the orthography changes, the meaning of the word, the implication of the past tense, remains the same in this instance. Secondly, Mama uses both "their" and "they." In Black English, "they" can be used as a possessive pronoun (Burling, 50). In the above passage, "they" assumes this connotation. Thirdly, and finally, Mama pronounces the word "about" as it is pronounced in Standard English *and* Black English ('bout). In Black English, words often lose the first syllable of a word when it is unstressed (Fasold, 51).

Why does Mama use these Black and Standard English synonyms? Perhaps this speech is merely reflective of a complex linguistic phenomenon which linguist Geneva Smitherman describes. She hypothesizes that the distance between Black and White English is not as great as it was in the past for several reasons. First, it is due to the extensive linguistic-cultural contact between Whites and Blacks and the inevitable cross-assimilation that is the result.[3]

On the other hand, it may reflect the code-switching which Blacks do occasionally. In America there is pressure upon minorities to speak Standard English in the work place, because Black English is a stigmatized dialect, and those who speak it are deemed uneducated and unemployable. But as Smitherman points out, the survival and persistence of Black dialect is due to the way in which the Black community exerts pressure upon its own members to speak "Black English" in intimate settings (because talking properly is not considered "cool"). Mama's speech may be reflective of what Smitherman calls the "push-pull" syndrome, "*pushing* toward White American culture while simultaneously *pulling* away from it" (11).

Is Mama consciously aware of "pushing and pulling" towards White America? This cannot be conclusively deduced from this passage, but it may be a possibility. Likewise, it is uncertain whether she usually speaks in Standard English or Black English. However, it is apparent in this passage that Mama is inclined to use Black English and she is also quite cognizant of Standard English; it is part of her bi-dialectal vocabulary.

Whether or not Mama is exercising a conscious awareness of her linguistic choices, the result of this textual mixture of Black and Standard English is playful and creative. Of course, Mama whines about the absence of milk, which she uses as a catalyst for complaining inappropriately about the financial burden she thinks Pecola has become. Such complaints are inappropriate because they make little Pecola responsible for a matter over which she has no control. However, the fact that Mama chastises Pecola in—not one, but *two* dialects—displays creativity. In hybridity lies the kind of juxtaposition of dialects which resembles a blending of spices.

It could be that Morrison deliberately chooses this playful dialectal hybridity to help make a poetic point. In other words, the language goes along with the playful, even humorous, posture: the idea that Mama will be sent to the poor house because of three quarts of milk; the ridiculous suspicion that people are conspiring to send her to the poor house; and the silly simile she uses to compare herself with a cat that has side pockets. Mama's words disguise a heart which is not capable of tossing Pecola out in the cold. As we discover later on in the narrative, no such thing happens. We can regard this passage, then, as a kind of hand-on-the-hip toughness which is simply a posture, a performance. And one of the components of this kind of performance is the hybridity, which helps to communicate the sense that even her dialect (Standard and/or Black) is at some level a playful performance. This playfulness mirrors the playful and sometimes performative nature of language use in the Black community. In both the literary and extra-literary realms, neither dialect maintains its purity and its innocence. Sometimes, each dialect allows itself to have intercourse with the "other" (dialect).

I choose the language of the prostitute Marie to further illustrate and develop my point.

"Hi *dumplin'*. *Where your socks?*" Marie seldom called Pecola the same thing twice . . . Must be *somethin'* in your house that *loves* socks" whenever something was

missing, Marie attributed its disappearance to "*something* in the house that loved it."
"*There is somethin'* in your house that *loves* brassieres," she would say. . . . (44)

As we can see, Marie has a habit of "dropping her g's," a feature of Black English in which the "in" suffix is substituted for the "ing" (Fasold, 55). Peculiarly, the narrator quotes her saying the same thing in both Standard English and Black dialect. She says both "somethin" and "something." Likewise, sometimes Marie deletes the verb to be and sometimes she does not. Linguist William Labov notes that where there is a contraction of "is" or "are" in Standard English, the verb "to be" is deleted in Black English (70). Marie follows this rule when she asks, "where your socks?" but she does not follow this rule when she says, "there is somethin . . ."

When I contrast Marie's speech with "Mama's," I notice several differences. For example, "Mama" does not drop her 'g's, as Marie does. On the other hand, "Mama" tends to leave out the third person singular "s," while Marie's speech does conform to this rule. When Marie says, for instance, "somethin' in your house that *loves*," she uses the standard "s" ending. In addition, Marie uses hypercorrection (when she says elsewhere, "They *wants* to put their toes in my curly hair" 45), which means that she uses the suffix "s" sporadically with present tense verbs other than the third person singular (Fasold, 64). This hypercorrection, too, distinguishes her speech from Mama's.

Morrison uses the rules for black dialect selectively and inconsistently in order to shape an idiosyncratic language for each character. Marie's hypercorrection and dropping of the "g's" distinguish her speech just as much as her use of the phrase, "whoa Jesus, ninety-nine!" (46). The overall effect of such idiosyncrasy, of course, means that features of Black English are not regularized and are, in effect, reduced. What do I mean when I say "reduced"? If Morrison had enforced the same grammatical rules for both Mama and Marie consistently, then there would be more features of Black English. Thus, this reduction is governed by the rules of characterization (the literary realm) as much as it is guided by the grammatical rules of the extra-literary realm which is reflected in bidialectical diversity of speech.

Now I wish to turn to the group of characters whose speech is most consistently Black. The first among these is Pauline, Pecola's mother. Morrison uses italics and quotation marks to represent Pauline's internal monologue.

"*When I first seed Cholly, I want you to know it was like all the bits of color from that time down home when all us chil'ren went berry picking after a funeral and I put some in the pocket of my Sunday dress, and they mashed up and stained my hips . . . and that lemonade Mama used to make . . . It be cool and yellowish, with seeds near the bottom. And that streak of green june bugs made on the trees the night we left down home. All of them colors was in me . . . [Cholly] used to whistle, and when I* heerd *him, shivers* come on my skin." *(91–92)*

Pauline's speech is consistently Black. There is a high concentration of Black English. Pauline's speech does not slip into Standard English (as Marie's and Mama's language does).

Morrison uses consistently Black grammatical and orthographical features in Pauline's language for a reason: they are deliberately chosen by Morrison as the best poetic vehicle to express a heightened sense of difference, alienation, and dis-ease that Pauline feels. One noticeable mark of dis-ease and alienation is her frequent use of hypercorrection. She uses "seed" and "heerd" as a non-standard past tense form of the irregular verbs, 'to see' and 'to hear.' Pauline knows that the past tense usually requires "ed" in Standard English and so she applies it, inappropriately, here. According to linguist Geneva Smitherman, hypercorrection is common among Black folks who "[try] to appropriate White English without the aid of specified grammatical rules . . ." (9). Her repeated use of hypercorrection marks her position as an outsider desperately trying to become an insider, one of those who has access to education and speaks English properly. Hypercorrection aligns her with a generation of Black folks who were marked by these linguistic signs of alienation.

Another sign of her difference is marked by orthography. She pronounces "children" according to the rules of Black English, which often demands that the "d" is deleted (Fasold, 54). The narrator tells us later (94) that Pauline was made fun of by her Black peers when she moved to the North from the South, because of the way she pronounced this word. "Their goading glances and private snickers at her way of talking (saying "chil'ren") and dressing developed in her a desire for new clothes" (94). Her pronunciation of "children" is obviously meant to signify a regional difference in Black dialect, since it was not a word common to her peers in the North. Thus, this word becomes a mark of geographical and linguistic difference and a stigma. Her use of this stigmatized language is so bothersome to Pauline, that the narrator remarks again that Pauline changes the way she pronounces the word "children": "She stopped saying "chil'ren" and said "childring" instead" (100). Unknowingly, Pauline has gone blindly down another lane in the labyrinth of hypercorrection.

Pauline uses an early form of Black English in this passage that further distinguishes her language from her peers. She uses the pronominal apposition construction in which a pronoun is used in apposition to the noun subject of the sentence. The phrase "It be cool," refers to the lemonade mentioned in the preceding sentence. Although the pronominal apposition construction usually takes place in a single sentence, I regard the two sentences as being part of one large sentence which has been separated according to nonstandard rules. According to Smitherman, when slaves learned English, they grafted some of their own West African language rules onto a form of Early Black English. One of these rules, which dictates a repetition of the noun subject with the pronoun still operates in Black English today (6). Pauline's use of this rule evokes the memory of this earlier linguistic moment of Earlier Black English, and makes a temporal distinction between her dialect and the dialect of the other characters.

Another signifier of Pauline's difference occurs when she uses "come" to indicate the past tense of the verb, "to come." In so doing, she uses a rare grammatical construction in Black English in which some verbs which have irregular past forms in Standard English have the same form for past and present tenses in Black dialect (Fasold, 60).

This dialect of alienation, difference, and dis-ease directly reflects Pauline's state of mind, which is best described by literary critic Susan Willis. What Willis says about another passage from Pauline (not quoted here) is applicable to the one I cite above:

> . . . in the grim and shabby reality of her present, orgasm (*which we might take as a metaphor for any deeply pleasurable experience*) is no longer possible. Living in a storefront, her husband fluctuating between brutality and apathy, her son estranged, her daughter just plain scared, Polly has no language to describe the memory of a past pleasure, except one drawn from her distant childhood. (83, emphasis mine)

Surely, Pauline's passage strikes one of the bluest notes in the novel. Her memory of the pleasure she derived from the sight of her husband, Cholly, when they first met, is couched in melancholy tones—and terms—because it is a paradise lost. Perhaps Pauline is no better off than the prostitute Marie, who, the narrator tells us, "hated all men" and "had no word for innocence" (47–48). Nor can we tell with any degree of certainty whether "Mama's fate is any better. Her past is never revealed, although clearly she is poor and working class. However, it is apparent that the jocular teasing and the story telling of the prostitutes and the tough talking posturing of "Mama" does not compare to the somber tone Pauline often assumes.

I turn to Leroi Jones' essay "Expressive Language," to help explain why Pauline's nigrosine tone is best reflected in her use of Black English. He says:

> . . . does clos-ter (in the context of "jes a close-ter, walk wi-thee") mean the same thing as closer? Closeter, in the term of the user is, believe me, exact. It means a quality of existence, of actual physical disposition perhaps . . . in its manifestation as a *tone* and

rhythm by which people live, most often in response to common modes of thought best
enforced by some factor of environmental emotion that is exact and specific. (328,
emphasis, his)

The condition of Pauline's life, her mood, and her existence as a Black
person living in that particular time and place, are part of what Jones' calls the
"environmental emotion," which shapes the form of Black English in general
and her monologue in particular.

When she recalls the memories she has of living down south before migrat-
ing north, her feelings of the loss of her idealized husband mix with the feelings
of loss she has for her idealized south as symbolized by the lemonade, the june
bugs, and the berry picking. Like thousands of other Blacks who left the south,
Pauline was deeply affected by her displacement.

But this "environmental emotion" is not simply affected by migration. It
is always/already affected by the African response to the middle passage and
slavery and sharecropping. Her black and blue notes deliberately recall
linguistically the historical experience of difference, alienation, displacement,
and dis-ease that Blacks have had in America before she was born. Hypercorrection and Early Black English were the products of this historical
experience; they live and evolve in her language.

The best example of a passage which expresses more of the character's
reality in its consistently Black English form than in its Standard English
equivalent occurs in the speech of Aunt Jimmy, Cholly's Great Aunt. When
Cholly asks her why she didn't name him after his father she responds:

What for? He wasn't nowhere around you when you was born. Your mama didn't name
you nothing. The nine days wasn't up before she throwed you on the junk heap. When
I got you I named you myself on the ninth day. You named after my dead brother.
Charles Breedlove. A good man. Ain't no Samson never come to no good end. (106)

Aunt Jimmy uses several examples of multiple negation in her language,
a construction peculiar to Black English. When translated into Standard English,
the multiple negation becomes a single negation. So "Ain't no Samson never
come to no good end," is the equivalent of the standard, 'There has never been
a Samson who came to a good end.' However, what's lost in that translation is
the emphatic sense and repetition of negation and the overwhelming feeling of
impossibility and pessimism that is implied. In addition, the Black English helps
Aunt Jimmy to communicate her razor sharp bluntness. The omission of the
verb "to be," for instance, shortens the following sentences: "You named after
my dead brother," and "A good man." These grammatical features combine with

the assonance created by a consistent use of the deeply mournful long "o." She uses "nowhere," "born," "nothing," "no," and "brother." In these examples, the consonant sound "n" is also because it signals through its repetition the importance of these words.

These visual cues mirror the meaning behind these words. In response to the universal question, "who am I?" Cholly's answer is nihilistic. Cholly is nobody. He came from no place. He was not wanted. His father and mother are nowhere to be found. He had no name. He is named after the dead. The Black English Aunt Jimmy uses to express this answer is blue(s).

Ironically, the last group of characters examined here who, along with Aunt Jimmy and Pauline, consistently speak Black English are the White characters. I cite two examples. The first example is the passage where a group of anonymous White hunters surprise Cholly when he is having his first sexual encounter with a young lady in the woods. With sinister glee, the hunters force him to continue this act, and in so doing, they become voyeurs of their own lasciviousness:

> "Come on, *coon*. Faster. You *ain't doing nothing* for her." . . . "Wait . . . the coon *ain't comed* yet . . . Well, *he have* to come on his own time. Good luck coon baby". (118)

There are several features of Black English used here. I have noted the presence of the first two features in the language of other (Black) characters. First, the hunters use multiple negation when they say, "ain't doing nothing." In the second sentence, two features are used. The term "ain't" is a popular Black English word for "has not." And "comed" is a form of hypercorrection, the irregular past tense of the verb "to come." Since the "ed" suffix is usually placed at the end of the past tense in Standard English, it has been used here as well. There is no sign that the hunters realize that the verb "to come" is irregular. The final use of Black English is documented by the linguist Fasold (66). The hunters delete the word, "will" from the sentence which implies future time: "he have to come on his own time."

The second instance in which Whites use Black English occurs shortly after this one. Cholly encounters a ticket salesperson at the bus station. He applies for the discount ticket sold to children. He lies about his age and his reason for traveling in order to convince the salesman that he qualifies for this ticket. Cholly is met with a response which combines insensitivity with kindness:

> "I reckon I *knows* a lying nigger when I *sees* one, but jest in case you ain't, jest in case one of *them* mammies is really dyin' and wants to see her little old smoke before she meets her maker, I *gone* do it." (121)

Like the hunters, the salesman also uses hypercorrection. When he says, "I knows," and "I sees," and "wants," he regularizes the third person singular suffix "s." The word, "ain't," is another feature which has been noted in Black English, as mentioned before. The use of "them" instead of "those," signifies the substitution of the objective pronoun for the demonstrative pronoun noted by critic Sylvia Holton as a feature of Black English (133). The salesman also drops his g's when he pronounces the word dying. And finally, he uses the future indicator "gonna" from the Black dialect to indicate the Standard English "going to" (Fasold, 65). Why is it that these White characters speak Black English? Could it be that there are no differences between southern White dialect and what we call Black dialect? This debate has been raging within the linguistic community for some time. A definitive answer has not yet been found. Yet, linguist Edgar Schneider, who has surveyed the literature, maintains that "most researchers would probably agree that black speech is to some extent different from the speech of whites even of a comparable socioeconomic and regional background, yet these differences, though consistent, are rather superficial . . ." (2).

In the language used by the hunters and the ticket salesman is an exhibition of linguistic similarity and feigned difference which marks the boundary here between Black and White southern dialect. The linguistic similarity is displayed in the grammatical features which make the race of the speaker indistinguishable. The feigned difference is in the lexicon. The derogatory expressions, "coon," and "nigger," and "old smoke" cannot be found either in the dictionary of Black English written by linguist Geneva Smitherman or the dictionary written by linguist Clarence Major. The words are peculiar to White (supremacist) lexicon. Ironically, these words signify the racial superiority and difference which is undermined by the appearance of Black English grammatical and orthographical structures. This linguistic irony mirrors the context of these passages. The Whites who disparage Cholly do so out of the misguided belief that they are different, when in fact, they are not. This feigned superior difference is the basis of their Whiteness. To highlight this dramatic irony, Morrison uses the linguistic irony: she has them speak Black English rather than a standard dialect which traditionally implies superior difference. Two effects result. First, the realm of poetry once again dictates a surprising turn of linguistic events. Secondly, the sound registered by this odd combination of Black dialect and White lexicon rings a discordant note in Morrison's song (text).

From the bass section of Black English, I move to other registers of sound to arrive at the third category of language. This shift marks an extraordinary linguistic event in which characters sustain highly polarized sounds: Black and Standard English. Little Pecola Breedlove presents a striking example; she speaks Standard English when she is insane and Black English when she is not insane. Her speech is different from the bi-dialectal display of Mama and Marie because her use of Black and Standard English are separated by time and space; she speaks these dialects at different times within the novel.

Although examples of Pecola's Black English can be found throughout the novel—with the exception, of course, of when she loses her mind—I focus on one particular passage for analysis here. Pecola speaks to her friends, Claudia and Frieda, about the prostitutes. I have placed Pecola's words in bold and underlined the words I call particular attention to:

> "**She _don't_ know I go. Miss Marie is nice. They _all_ nice.**" Oh, yeah," I said, "she tried to kill us." "**Who? Miss Marie? She _don't bother nobody._**" "Then how come your mama don't let you go in her house if she so nice?" "**I don't know. She _say_ she's bad, but they _ain't_ bad.**". (85)

In Black dialect, the "s" suffix is deleted from the word, "don't" in the present tense when the subject is in the third person singular (Fasold, 63). Such is the case when Pecola states: "She don't know I go," instead of the standard, 'she doesn't know I go.' The verb "to be" is missing from her declaration, "They all nice." She uses the familiar multiple negation in her sentence, "she don't bother nobody." She loses the third person suffix "s" in "she say she's bad. . ." Finally, Pecola uses the omnipresent "ain't."

Contrast Pecola's language here with the language she uses in the last chapter when she goes mad. In this passage, she imagines that she gets what she has always wanted: a pair of blue eyes which symbolize her acceptance in a White world which demeans her Black skin and culture. To convey the onslaught of this new blindness, Morrison depicts a scene in which Pecola has a conversation with an imagined friend whose words are rendered in italics (Morrison's emphasis). Absent from her syntax are the markers of Black dialect. She omits multiple negation and the word "ain't" from her lexicon; and she uses subject-verb agreement and the verb "to be":

> You're just jealous.
> _I am not._
> You are. You wish you had them.
> _Ha. What would I look like with blue eyes?_ (150, emphasis, hers)

This conversation evokes the image of a hall of mirrors. First, it represents Pecola's divided mind externalized. Her new-found friend verbalizes the doubt Pecola has about her new eyes when she mocks this prized possession. Secondly, the friend functions as a mirror, not of conscience, but of imagined admiration, when Pecola refuses to consider the words of sarcasm and dissent. Finally, there is a linguistic mirror. The conversation mimics dialogue without ever becoming it. After all, since the friend is not real, perhaps this conversation does not exist in the form it assumes on the page. Pecola's conversation is not in quotations, so readers cannot rule out the possibility that this conversation is a linguistically ordered representation of the unspeakable and unspoken unconscious thoughts held in Pecola's mind.[4] Thus, Morrison holds a mirror to the (backward) chaotically dispersed words and creates order for the readers.

Pecola's language thus articulates linguistically the chaotic psychological experience of seeing this self through the eyes of White society, which Michael Awkward (with a nod to Dubois' concept of double consciousness) calls "schizophrenic double voicedness."[5] Awkward uses this term to describe the point at which she sees herself, permanently, through the eyes of White society.[6] I would expand Awkward's concept to add that this shift in Pecola's mental vision is accompanied by her linguistic acquisition of two voices. Not only are there the two voices (hers and her "friends") to which Awkward's "double voices" refer, but there are also the two dialects, Standard and Black English, which Pecola uses before her madness, and during her madness. The Standard English voice marks a permanent shift that Awkward observes; a shift in which her self is literally torn apart, and her self is permanently criticized and judged through the eyes of the racist Other (the metaphor of the linguistic mirrors poetically conveys the idea of seeing and reflecting a disjointed Other).

Mae Henderson's trope on "speaking in tongues" further edifies Pecola's utterances in double tongues (Black and Standard English). Henderson acknowledges that her term "speaking in tongues," comes from the Book of Acts which describes how the Holy Spirit fills the Disciples of Christ with language heretofore unknown to them. This miraculous act signifies communion with God. As Henderson suggests, speaking in tongues, both the ability to speak in diverse tongues recognizable to man and the ability to speak in a private tongue recognizable to God. Likewise, Pecola speaks a private language which, like the "tongues" is for a single audience (herself). And to expand on this concept of tongues in order to further explicate this text, I refer to Romans, chapter eight, which says, "the Spirit itself maketh intercession for us with groanings which cannot be uttered." The Holy Spirit gives utterance to those things which are unspoken and unspeakable. Likewise, in Standard English, Pecola finally gives utterance to the unspeakable. What is the main (literary) purpose of speaking in tongues?

Henderson suggests that Black women in general and Black women writers in particular, develop multiple voices, the glossolalia and the heteroglossia, in order to discourse with the Other. She writes:

> Black women writers enter into testimonial [familiar] discourse with black men as blacks, with white women as women, and with black women as black women. At the same time they enter into a competitive discourse with black men as women, with white women as blacks, and with white women as black women. (20)

In using two dialects for Pecola, Morrison addresses, simultaneously, Blacks and Whites. Earmarked boldly in Standard English is the fact of Pecola's purchase of the Other's vision of herself, a detrimental and insane act which is never before explicit (as insanity), and which is veiled in Black English discourse. Astute readers of all colors will understand Pecola's message in Black and Standard English. But it may be that the dialects specifically acknowledge Morrison's openly competitive and contestatory discourse with Whites in Standard English and her coded and familial discourse with Blacks in Black English.

The use of Standard English to distinguish an occasion or character gone horribly wrong occurs throughout the novel. The Dick and Jane primer in the epigraph is a case in point. Like the implied universe of the narrator, the excerpt from the primer reflects a universe in which life appears to be perfect. This primer is rendered in the same Standard English used by the narrator:

> Here is the house. It is green and white. It has a red door. It is very pretty. Here is the family. Mother, Father, Dick, and Jane live in the green-and-white house. They are very happy . . . Mother will you play with Jane? Mother laughs . . . Father, will you play with Jane? Father smiles. (7)

According to Michael Awkward, the universe presented in this paragraph is a myth. Its status as myth, Awkward argues, is apparent when Morrison contrasts this epigraph with the story of Pecola. The story's ability to speak the truth about reality is undermined by its distance and difference from Afro-American reality. Pecola's abusive and emotionally distant family can never compare to the idealized Dick and Jane family in the primer.

On the other hand, even the Dick and Jane family has problems beneath the smooth, happy surface of their idealized lives, as Awkward points out. After all, he argues, "The emotional estrangement of the primer family members (an estrangement suggested by that family's inability to respond to the daughter Jane's desire for play) implies that theirs is solely a surface contentment" (61). The language of the primer reflects an ironic situation which levels a critique against what Awkward calls the "bourgeois myths of ideal family life," while doing so unselfconsciously, as if in a dense, white fog of Standard English.

A rupture in the Standard English of the Dick and Jane story also appears in the epigraph. In this rupture, Morrison squeezes together the words of the Dick and Jane story, rendering a perfectly Standard English nonstandard. In so doing, Morrison dramatizes *linguistically* what occurs *conceptually*. Like the play Shakespeare's Hamlet designs to describe the murder he suspects as a kind of play within a play, acting out the break down of the bourgeois myth of the ideal family before it happens. Here is a sample of this linguistic play from the epigraph:

Hereisthehouseitisgreenandwhiteithasareddooritisverypretty
Hereisthefamilymotherfatherdickandjaneliveinthegreenhouse
Theyareveryhappy . . . motherwillyouplaywithjanemotherlaughs
Fatherwillyouplaywithjanefatherissmiling . . . (8)

The rupture which occurs here is used to signify a blue(s) house of stark reality which interrupts the fog of fantasy, holding clouds of double consciousness, signified by Standard English.

The language of Pecola's schoolmate, Maureen, is another case in point. Maureen is the middle-class Black girl who represents the double consciousness of the idealized bourgeois who have lost touch with the epigraph that occurs in her speech: her nearly perfect Standard English breaks down.

While Maureen walks home from school with Pecola, Claudia, and Frieda, she unwittingly makes comments which dishonor her friends and her own Black community. In a language which is certainly much closer to the standard than that of most of the other characters, she casually talks about the depiction of race in a movie: "The picture show . . . Where this mulatto girl hates her mother 'cause she is black and ugly but then cries at the funeral. It was real sad." (57) Maureen misses the irony. Maureen, who is described as a bourgeois, "high-yellow dream child," is apparently just like the mulatto in the movie: she hates dark-skinned people. This hatred is so commonplace among her own thoughts, that she cannot recognize it. Instead, she adopts a posture of difference and distance from other Blacks, and as a result, is guilty of looking upon them through the eyes of a racist society.

Maureen stumbles along blindly after she makes this comment. Soon enough, she makes another remark which demonstrates how deeply she has absorbed the derogatory insults hurled at her friend Pecola from her father. Long after the boys who issue the offending remarks have left, Maureen asks, "Did you ever see a naked man?" (59). But this time, when Maureen raises the specter of this insult, she is confronted head on by Claudia and Frieda. They force her to acknowledge the lack of difference and distance between her and Pecola by pointing out that her comments reflect her own state of mind. Together, they remind Maureen that all she talks about is "boys, babies, and somebody's naked daddy." Like a soprano who suddenly breaks into deep, base, blue notes, Maureen acquires the anger that comes from the rupture of her fantasy world, and changes the color of her dialect. She hurls an insult at Frieda and drops her copula: "You all ready made. Mammy made" (60). She drops it again when she screams her parting insult: "I am cute! And you ugly! Black and ugly . . ." (61).

Maureen's language does not simply don a Black grammatical coat, it also joins in an ancient linguistic game performed in the Black community, called "playing the dozens." In this game, as critic Claudia Mitchell-Kernan explains, "insults include derogatory remarks about the family of the addressee, particularly [her] mother" (317). In this context, Maureen's comment that her friends were made by their mothers (which is, of course, true) becomes an insult, Maureen engages in "sounding." Mitchell-Kernan notes that it is closely related to "playing the dozens." It is simply a form of a direct verbal insult (sound) which does not refer to members of the family (316–317). In short, Maureen's language blushes in more ways than one when she is reminded that she is no different from Pecola.

In a bizarre reversal (or repetition) of this phenomenon of rupturing, Pecola imagines her parents, Cholly and Pauline Breedlove, speaking Standard English. These are the circumstances under which Pecola produces this wish:

> It had occurred to Pecola some time ago that if her eyes . . . were different, that is to say, beautiful, she herself would be different. Her teeth were good, and at least her nose was not big and flat like some of those who were thought so cute. If she looked different, beautiful, maybe Cholly would be different, and Mrs. Breedlove too. Maybe they'd say, "Why look at pretty-eyed Pecola. We mustn't do bad things in front of those pretty eyes." (40)

An examination of Cholly and Pauline's language demonstrates that they are not speakers of Standard English. The analysis of Pauline's language at the beginning of this chapter shows that she uses features of Black English more consistently than many of the other characters in the novel. Cholly rarely speaks, and when he does, he always uses Black English. (I will analyze Cholly's speech at length below.)

Why is it that Pecola imagines her parents using Standard English? Standard English, once again, signifies the fantasy world of those with blue eyes. It is the language of the Dick and Jane primer which describes the White family who never seem to have any problems. Ironically, when Pecola imagines her parents speaking Standard English, its congruity with their patterns of speech is striking and odd. In other words, I think the language, which falls on the ears like a harsh, brass note, signifies the danger—and the deceptiveness—of equating the status of unattainable Whiteness with perfection. It is precisely because Pecola attributes her problems to her physical lack (symbolized here by the color of her eyes) that she is not able to *see* that her problems stem from her mental attitude: her belief that she is wanting, that she is unattractive, and that she is racially inferior.

There is one character in the novel who never leaves the fog of insanity and *always* speaks Standard English. He is in a class by himself. That character is Soaphead, the child molester and misanthrope who "gives" Pecola her blue eyes by convincing her that they can turn blue. He explains why in an angry letter to God:

> . . . Not for pleasure, and not for money. I did what You did not, could not, and would not do: I looked at that ugly little black girl, and I loved her. I played You. And it was a very good show. (143)

Soaphead gives Pecola much more than blue eyes. He reinforces her way of seeing. He thinks she is ugly and that her ugliness is due to her physical features instead of her mental attitude. We see that once Pecola buys Soaphead's message, not only does she get completely lost in his mental fog, but even acquires his syntax, grammatical, and orthographical features.[7] All the while, the layer of irony which laces Pecola's insanity speech is apparent in Soaphead's also: Soaphead thinks he is playing God while he plays the devil.

Does Standard English take on the same meaning in all of the characters who use it? The answer is no. In the case of Claudia the narrator, who speaks Standard English when she is older and Black English when she is younger, the language reflects a realistic (rather than literary and imaginative) change which reflects the passing of time and the attainment of education. The following passage in which Claudia remembers a past experience, the text demonstrates the contrast between Claudia (the older and wiser) narrator, and Claudia the (younger) little girl. I place in bold Claudia's words, and underline the words I wish to call particular attention to:

> **They [the boys] had extemporized a verse made up of two insults about matters over which the victim had no control: the color of her skin and speculations on the**

sleeping habits of an adult, wildly fitting in its incoherence. That they themselves were black, or that their own father had similarly relaxed habits was irrelevant . . . "You shut up, Bullet Head." I had found my tongue . . . You want a fat lip?" "Yeah. *Gimme* one of yours." . . . "*Old Bullet Head, He's always* picking on girls." (55–56)

In young Claudia's speech, there is pronoun apposition, whereby she repeats the subject, "Old Bullet Head," with the pronoun "he." Secondly, deletes the consonant "v" from the end of the word, "give." Pronounced quickly, it sounds like, "gimme." The reader is drawn to the eloquent, studied thoughts communicated through the narrator's Standard English. In fact, the thoughts of Claudia as a narrator are more astute and perceptive than Claudia as actor-speaker. The narrator witnesses the irony of the situation in which the boys use Pecola as a scapegoat to mask and relieve their own feelings of anxiety and worthlessness concerning their skin color and their fathers'. Claudia the speaker never betrays this awareness, but instead, her comments reflect the same childish display of cockiness and false bravado displayed by the boys. She never bothers to explain to them, in Black English, the adult, sophisticated thoughts she holds as a narrator. However, this does not mean that Claudia does not sense that something is wrong. The narrator carefully points out that Claudia stands up for Pecola, and does what is right, even though she does not articulate (with the clarity of the narrator) the reasons for her anger.

In a sense, then, the younger and the older Claudia are of one accord. And neither the speaker nor the narrator at any point engages in the kind of double consciousness which holds the boys (who speak Black English) in thrall. The fact that Claudia and the boys' use of language reverse the reader's expectations that Standard English comes to signifiy double consciousness is consistent with Morrison's deviate from literary and linguistic expectations. In this instance, Morrison proves that Claudia's acquisition of Standard English does not distance her from the point of view of her youth. And it certainly does not alienate her from her culture. Instead, Claudia's understanding has only improved with age. Indeed, it is Claudia as narrator who unearths the secrets of Pecola's demise at the hands of her community and her culture. Her razor sharp (re) vision of what happened only heightens our sense of her rebellion, as a child, against a culture that sought to make her dislike herself (as it does with Pecola). As critic Susan Willis points out, "Claudia is the renegade . . . [she is] the representation of a stance that Afro-Americans in general might take against white domination" (174).

If Claudia is the renegade, the epitome of physical rebellion channeled positively and powerfully into razor-sharp words, if her words are examples of using the master's tools (writing and Standard English) to dissemble the master's house, then Cholly Breedlove is her opposite. He is never able to articulate the source of his anger, and, in fact, instead of expressing himself verbally, he relies on the language of his body to speak for him. In the following passage,the narrator interprets Cholly's thoughts when he is about to rape his daughter:

> Cholly saw her dimly and *could not tell* what he saw or what he felt. Then he became aware that he was uncomfortable; next he felt the Dissolve into pleasure. The sequence of his emotions was revulsion, Guilt, pity, then love. (127, My emphasis)

Cholly's language, like Soaphead's, occupies a category unto itself. His language is unspeakable and unspoken because it is pure feeling and action. The narrator goes on to show how his feelings of revulsion, pity, and love, spur his actions as he reads the language of her body and responds with his: "her back hunched that way; her head to one side . . . why did she have to look so whipped?" (127). He reads the love and "hauntedness" in her eyes and feels irritated. He wants his hands to produce a smile. Crawling towards her, he tries to force a laugh from her and instead rapes her—reacting wildly to his desire. In Cholly's language we read Soaphead's misguided message to God. Both men insist upon "fixing" the body and ignoring the soul.

I think Cholly's silence can be compared to Pecola's insane use of Standard English. The silence represents the inability of language to express the reason why Cholly behaves as he does. Morrison takes pains to show us that Cholly, like Pecola, is the fullest realization of absence, negation, and lack which can occur in people who have been oppressed. Pecola's rape is prefaced by a full explanation by the narrator of how Cholly became himself. In addition to his abandonment by his parents and the death of his caretaker and the absence of a social network which could protect him and guide him—in addition to this, Cholly was deeply affected by the White hunters who forced him to rape his girlfriend. The rape of Pecola mirrors the sense of impotence and inferiority he felt during his first sexual experience. Spoken language cannot express the chaos of Cholly's feelings, just as language represents Pecola's chaotic thoughts. However, music, like Morrison's linguistic mirror for Pecola, can express the essence of Cholly. The narrator tells us:

> The pieces of Cholly's life could become coherent only in the head of a musician. Only those who talk their talk through the gold of curved metal, or in the touch of black-and-white rectangles and taut skins and strings echoing from wooden corridors, could give true form to his life. (125)

In the passages which express Cholly's insane act and Pecola's insanity, Morrison challenges and expands the boundaries of the reader's expectations for the characters' relationship to language. Morrison does this when she uses language to describe what is unspeakable and unspoken in musical terms (for Cholly) or (for Pecola) in Standard English rather than in Black English. She does it again when she has Pecola to imagine her parents using Standard English when they usually speak (and the reader expects) Black English. In so doing, its look—grammar and syntax—becomes much more than the reader expects. It becomes an utterance which fails to hold the character in a fixed relationship with "race"and/or "class." In the case of Marie and Mama, their use of a mixed form of Black English and Standard English raises questions about the extent to which the linguistic choices they make are reflective of bi-dialectal minds. Or one can consider the narrator Claudia who speaks in two dialects; the ease with which she moves in and out of these dialects recalls an actor using two different masks. The looks also acquire the symbolic power of a mask when forced to communicate meaning which is not usually explicitly carried in the linguistic sign: the use of Standard English as a signifier of double consciousness. In the ways aforementioned, the language is at play in the sense that it is not used to replicate 'real' Black English (extra-literary), but it is at the mercy of the forces which shape a whimsical literary world.

Paradoxically, the language within this novel is not playing. It's whipped, beaten, and molded by extra-literary forces when it is made to conform to reality. Its features are the spitting image of present, past, and future "real life." We are reminded here of the language that comes from Polly's lips which could have been uttered by our own African ancestors. And Claudia's (as well as Mama's, and Marie's) transition from Black to Standard English—and her easy transition between them in the novel—reflects the bi-dialectal changes which have come when Blacks gained access to education.

As a result of this push and pull of literary and extra-literary forces acting upon language, it develops a lively personality, part of which is revealed by the analysis of this chapter. Sometimes, the language has to get down on its knees and admit that it cannot represent a character's reality, as it does in the case of Pecola. Sometimes, all it can do is sing or hum, as it does with Cholly. The music and the silence, too, imitate language: they reflect reactions to those occasions which remain unspeakable and unspoken, and are valid terms of this peculiar Black lexicon.

The aforementioned ways in which language is used to articulate richly, inventively, and manipulatively the relationship between these Black characters and language itself are what I call Black **acts**. Surprisingly, these Black linguistic acts include events which use the **looks** of Standard English to accomplish, guerilla style, its mission.

· 2 ·

THE EVIDENCE OF THINGS UNSEEN[1]:
THE SHAPE OF ORALITY IN
THE BLUEST EYE

Toni Morrison's *The Bluest Eye* addresses the question of how to tell its story in Black English, using writing to suggest the presence of a dialect most often used orally.[2] Morrison explains (and evaluates the effectiveness of) how this rhetorical manipulation of words is used to suggest and infuse orality into the written word. This explanation reveals the **acts** which makes language Black:

> . . . my choices of language (speakerly, aural, colloquial), my reliance for full compre-
> hension on codes embedded in black culture, my effort to immediate co-conspiracy and

intimacy (without distancing, explanatory fabric), as well as my (failed) attempt to shape a silence while breaking it are attempts (many unsatisfactory) to transfigure the complexity and wealth of Afro-American culture into a language worthy of the culture. (23)[3]

In the last chapter, I explained how the dialogue in this novel suggests a communicative realm which is speakerly, aural, colloquial. I examined the extent to which the words were made to resemble the sound of Black English through the arrangement of its grammar, syntax, and spelling. In this chapter, I examine how the words convey the atmosphere surrounding Black English through its structures of rhetoric and narrative. Eric Havelock's definition of orality pinpoints the aspects I cover in this chapter. To paraphrase Havelock's definition, the term "orality" suggests the language used in oral communication, the consciousness created and expressed by oral communication, and the kind of community expressed by oral communication, and the kind of community which relies on oral rather than written communication (11). I analyze the way in which the words in this novel are made to suggest the consciousness of the realms of orality—the conspiracy, intimacy, and silence which occur between an through the exchange of words within the universe of the *The Bluest Eye*. Thus, the language reveals the atmosphere of intimacy and conspiracy which forges the community that surrounds Pecola Breedlove and her family, and juxtaposes these unwritten ties that bind against the silence and alienation which surrounds and defines the discourse of the Breedloves.

The set of conversations analyzed in this chapter reveals Morrison's experimentation—not failure, as she modestly asserts—with rhetorical maneuvers designed to use the written language to depict or suggest what only occurs in the oral realm of the community; and in the case of the Breedloves, what does not occur at all. This experimentation gives birth to an unconventional written discourse which speaks—gives voice to—the unspoken and even unconscious response of the Breedloves to their alienation and despair. In effect, Morrison creates a literary representation of what has only been spoken orally (or occurred only in the oral realm) within the African American culture, and represents what has been too traumatic to speak at all.

These unconventional literary representations are partial, eclipsed conversations which blur the boundaries of what is oral and what is written as each conversation both contests and confirms its existence as a "spoken" entity which indicates that which is voiced (but unspoken) and that which is spoken (or occurs only in the realm of the unspoken).

This occurs in several ways. Some events reveal a partially constructed conversation. Some events contain a false record of spoken conversations. Some events hide conversations in the narrative. Some events look like written representations of conversation, but actually describe unspoken thoughts. And some events mention conversations which are not represented on the page and only occur in the realm of orality. The content of these events is as surreptitious as its form; each bespeaks confidential, unfamiliar, and untold occasions. My analysis also reveals the iterability of many of these conversations: this repetition suggests a controlled, defined universe of communication which routinely excludes the Breedloves. The shape of this language—how it **looks** on the page—unfolds the continuum between the oral and the written; paradoxically, it also reveals the distinction between the separate worlds of the oral and the written.

I begin my analysis with a dialogue in which the words written on the page are not exact replicas of the words which occur in the spoken conversation it represents. I refer to the gossip which Mrs. MacTeer (Claudia's mother) exchanges with her friends about her new roomer, Mr. Henry, and his associates. What is peculiar—and even bizarre—about this discussion is that the narrator, Claudia, intervenes with a side comment, halfway through, and informs readers rather casually that "Frieda and I are washing Mason jars. *We do not hear their words*, but with grown-ups we listen to and watch out for their voices" (emphasis mine, 15). To underscore this message, Claudia informs the readers "*We do not, cannot, know the meanings of all their words*, for we are nine and ten years old" (emphasis mine, 16). How is it, then, that Mrs. MacTeer's talk comes equipped with quotation marks? Why would Claudia lead us to believe that her mother speaks these words?

The words we see before us on the page are a representation of dialogue filtered through the consciousness of the narrator as a young child and an older adult. Claudia tells the story using her childhood memories, and when those memories are inadequate, she uses her adult imagination. The conversation described here reveals the boundaries between these two vantage points. Claudia remembers the conversation, but must imagine the details of its contents.[4] It is given quotation marks and is stuffed with filler words so that the reader's imagination can be stimulated as well. The content of Mrs. MacTeer's gossip remains unspoken, because what she actually says to her cohorts is never revealed to the narrator and to readers. Morrison's construction of dialogue here allows for an unusual reading experience: readers are given a fully detailed picture of a conversation and then are told that it is not accurate. As a result, readers are made aware of the impoverishment of the written word compared to the spoken.

In addition, Claudia calls upon readers to use what is written on the page to recall qualities associated solely with oral communication. She observes:

> Their conversation is like a gently wicked dance: sound meets sound, curtsies, shimmies, and retires. Another sound enters but is upstaged by still another: the two circle each other and stop. Sometimes their words move in lofty spirals; other times they take strident leaps, and all of it is punctuated with warm-pulsed laughter—like the throb of a heart made of jelly. The edge, the curl, the thrust of their emotions is always clear to Frieda and me . . . we watch their faces, their hands, their feet, and listen for truth in timbre. (16)

The imagery Claudia uses of a lively dance fittingly describes the movement of words in oral conversation. The way the speakers interact when they speak and the way in which their words connect during the conversation are the aspects of oral communication which Claudia wants her audience to focus on. I cite an excerpt from Mrs. MacTeer's gossip in order to review these aspects:

> "You know him," she [Mrs. MacTeer] said to her friends. "Henry Washington. He's been living over there with Miss Della Jones on Thirteenth Street. But she's too addled now to keep up. So he's looking for another place." "Oh yes." Her friends do not hide their curiosity. "I been wondering how long he was going to stay up there with her. They say she's real bad off. Don't know who he is half the time, and nobody else." (14)

Critic Deborah Tannen's analysis of dialogue in her book, *Conversational Style*, can be used here to consider the patterns of this conversation. Tannen notes the presence of what she calls "linguistic devices," which characterize the ebb and flow of conversation; such devices mirror shared and individual consciousness (how they feel about one another and about that of which they speak) of the speakers. The existence of these devices in the conversation on the page indicates the kind of interaction between speakers which can only occur off the page during oral communication.

Examples of such devices abound. The gossip reflects the participants' mutual choice of intimate, personal topics. As Tannen argues, this choice, as opposed to the choice of the more distant and distancing topics, reflects a willingness to be open to communicate (54–58). As well, the exchange is marked by what Tannen calls "cooperative prompting" (118). When Mrs. MacTeer offers information on Mr. Henry, her friends respond with a cooperative, encouraging word, "Oh, yes." And the personal statement volunteered by Mrs. MacTeer is met with "mutual revelation." Other such statements, which are similarly personal and intimate, are volunteered by her friends (79). The fact that this dialogue does not report who is, in fact, speaking (whether Mrs. MacTeer or her friends) is in itself suggestive of other devices. The lack of boundaries between words is reminiscent of those occasions when utterances from different speakers "overlap" and "latch" on to one another at a fast pace (77–78).

The existence of these devices in Mrs. MacTeer's conversation gives evidence to the structure of linguistic movement and feeling Claudia describes when speaks of the "gently wicked dance" and the "shimmies" of the dialogue. What Claudia describes is the aura which surrounds the words. This aura is produced, and signaled, by the particular linguistic devices chosen by the speakers. Tannen summarizes this phenomenon best when she says:

> . . . the degree to which one's meaning is understood as intended depends upon the degree to which conversational strategies, and hence the use of devices, are similar. Furthermore, the similarity of such devices makes for rhythmically smooth interaction. Both the rhythmic synchrony and the construction of shared meaning create the satisfying sense of harmony that often accompanies conversation among people who share the same social, ethnic, geographic, or class background. (150)

The conversational style of Mrs. MacTeer, her choices of linguistic devices, matches perfectly with those of her friends. Her willingness to be familiar and intimate, the rhythm of her speech, the connection of her syntax with those of others, and a whole host of other devices which we readers can only imagine[5]: the pitch and the gestures—are all choices which not only reflect her emotional harmony but her linguistic harmony with her friends. These linguistic choices comprise Claudia's description of the "wicked dance": and establishes an aura of consciousness produced by shared linguistic style and mutual understanding which is never uttered but is communicated in the realm of orality. Tannen muses: "The satisfaction of shared rhythm, shared appreciation of nuance, mutual understanding that surpasses the meaning of words exchanged . . . goes beyond the pleasure of having one's meaning understood. It is a ratification of one's way of being human . . ." (152). Surely it is the celebration of shared linguistic style and the aura of intimacy it produces which Claudia calls our attention to.

Claudia's written description of this exchange, and even the imprint of its structure in this conversation, does not do justice to that which occurs in the physical realm of interaction in oral communication. As a result, the written word in this conversation interacts with the spoken word from two vantage points which appear paradoxical. The conversation impresses some of the rhetorical structures of orality in order to replicate it. In so doing, the written and the spoken exist in continuum, where their boundaries are not separate. At the same time, the written word as it appears in Claudia's description can only describe, rather enviously, what occurs in orality. In so doing, the boundaries between written and spoken become fixed as the written draws attention to the kind of communication which does not take place within its boundaries. What is spoken in this linguistic event—and by this, I mean what is revealed—is one of the structures of orality; but its contents remain silent.

The silence of these contents makes creative demands upon the reader who is aware of its presence. The pitch, pace, facial gestures, and the words must be drawn from the imaginative mind of the reader to construct a conversation which exists in a creative universe parallel to the one created by the conversation on the page. Readers may rely upon their own imagination and memory to construct this universe.[6] I imagine Mrs. MacTeer half whispering her words playfully. I remember the physical feelings of comfort and titillation which surround words that trace a thin line between brutal truth and malicious criticism. Those feelings surge into facial muscles, hands, and feet and communicate movements both urgent and relaxed. There are the age old words of gossip and which resonate in my own memories of gossip. The familiarity of these words makes it easy for readers to meet the imaginative demands of the text because the linguistic event is so common to everyday experiences.[7] And not only does the text call to mind the individual consciousness which occurs during this kind of oral conversation, but, as Karla Holloway points out, the collective consciousness of a culture which commonly produces such conversations of a culture which commonly produces such conversations also comes to mind. She observes that the "wicked dance" recalls those "archaic" languages in Africa, which are primarily oral, and not written. Such languages are "archaic" because:

> they create significance by bringing into consciousness and *being* the heretofore unconscious. It is as if language is reaching back towards a reality that is only accessible through verbal symbolism—whether or not the symbol is artistic (as in the gently wicked dance) or musical (the children listening to their mother's conversation for "truth in timbre"), the imagery of the linguistic, and is reliable, because it is drawn from archaism. (39)

What Morrison achieves through the imagery suggested by writing, is the depiction of a kind of communication which carries linguistic memory. This memory triggers in Holloway the memory of race and place: the cultural imprint of Africa and its ways of communicating upon Black communities in America.

Aside from the dual creative process encouraged by the silence, the presence of the unspoken in this linguistic event serves a thematic function. The character of Mr. Henry is introduced in a cloud of sexual secrets.[8] And even though they are not about him, they foreshadow his underhanded nature. The talk about Della, who does not "smell" like a woman subtly conceals preferences for women who emit sexual smells. This secret hints at Mr. Henry's 'nasty' preferences for women. It is revealed later that he sleeps with prostitutes and makes advances towards Frieda, Claudia's ten-year-old sister.[9]

A related theme introduced by the silence in this context is the alienation caused by secrets. The bond of friendship, the verbal interaction, and the tangible rapport between Mrs. MacTeer and her friends bespeaks a strong knit linguistic community in this circle of friends. Not only do they share linguistic devices and classified information, but they share a familiarity with names and places, and they share common values. In short, the very thing which is enacted but not revealed here is a community shaped and linked by their words.[10] Readers are excluded from this linguistic community because, after all, we do not know what they are talking about. But others, too, are excluded. Pecola and her family, whose silences lie at the center of this novel, are never mentioned in Mrs. MacTeer's conversation.[11] So the gossip shows, by omission, what is missing from the lives of the Breedloves. Their names are not mentioned in the linguistic community described here, nor do they ever have the kind of rapport, that unspoken feeling of belonging, which comes with being understood.

In contrast to this linguistic event, which details a conversation whereby none of the words written on the page represent actual words spoken in the oral realm, there is another kind of event in which only some of the words written on the page in the oral realm. I call this kind of event partial representation. Such is the case with Mrs. MacTeer's diatribe against Pecola.[12] Although a sizable portion of Mrs. MacTeer's words are written, Morrison makes use of ellipses to indicate words that were never transcribed. For example, the dialogue begins with ellipses, ". . . I don't know what I'm suppose to be running here, a charity ward, I guess" (23). Mrs. MacTeer's monologue is interrupted by the narrator, Claudia, who indicates that she stops listening to her mother. At this point, the conversation ends. But it is again recorded after Claudia's remarks, beginning again with ellipses, ". . . and here I am poor as a bowl of yak-me" (24). The written fragments simulate Claudia's act of listening to her mother off and on.

Even though she does not hear the words, Claudia draws our attention to the structure of her mother's monologue, just as she draws our attention to the structure of her mother's gossip. Between excerpts from the monologue, Claudia describes its structure:

> My mother's fussing soliloquies always irritated and depressed us. They were interminable . . . She would go on like that for hours, connecting one offence to another until all of the things that chagrined her were spewed out. Then having told everybody and everything off, she would burst into song . . . (23)

What differentiates the structure described here from the structure described in the gossip is that Claudia explicitly reveals that the soliloquy is repeated. No such claims are made for the gossip, although the argument can be made that the written (material) evidence of the structure itself is an implicit revelation of the event's iterability. We can only say for certain that Mrs. MacTeer's gossip does not occur more than once in this literary world: but its apparent structure always lets the readers know that the gossip is not alien to the linguistic universe of the MacTeers. The soliloquy, on the other hand, is illuminated differently by the revelation of its structure. First, readers are presented with Mrs. MacTeer's attack on Pecola, a speech which appears to be singular. Then, readers are struck by the predictability of Mrs. MacTeer's diatribe when Claudia says, "When Mama got around to Henry Ford and all those people who did not care whether she had a loaf of bread, it was time to go" (24). These words make regular appearances in Mrs. MacTeer's soliloquies. They constitute its structure, along with the songs which come at the end. Critic Gerard Genette places such a narrative in the category of a "singulative" mode merging with an interactive mode (114). The singulative mode describes a narrated event that occurs once. This is certainly the case with Mrs. MacTeer's response to Pecola when she drinks three quarts of milk. This response is geared to the particular moment of this event: it is not repeated again in the course of the novel. However, this particular response merges with familiar, repeated words, concerning, for example, Henry Ford. And the way in which Mrs. MacTeer links her response to Pecola with other, older grievances is what Genette calls iterative, a repetitive narrative.

Tannen's research on formulaic language can be used here to discover the place of the iterative and singulative narratives in the realm of orality. Formulaic language includes fixed expressions which are used often. One example includes cliches, age old sayings which purport to contain wisdom. Another example is the language used in specific situations (she gives the example of saying "goodbye" before hanging up the phone).[13] In the excerpt from The Bluest Eye, Mrs. MacTeer's conversation begins to take on the dimensions of formulaic language when it becomes iterative, when she uses the words always reserved for such diatribes. Claudia notes the emergence of this language, when her mother talks about Henry Ford.

On the other hand, the novelty of the language Mrs. MacTeer uses to address Pecola in the singulative mode gives utterance to a language which is at variance with formulaic language. What is the relationship between oral and literate realms if formulaic language is associated with the oral and novel language with the written?[14] In one way, they can be viewed as inseparable.

Tannen argues that ". . . [the] literate tradition does not replace the oral . . . Rather . . . the two are superimposed and intertwined with each other . . . people use devices associated with both [oral and literate] in various settings" (3). If, as Tannen suggests, the formulaic language exists on a continuum upon which the other end is original syntactic patterns, then this passage from *The Bluest Eye* can be placed on a continuum. When Mrs. MacTeer's message addresses Pecola and new, singulative language is used, it can be said that this language takes on more of an element of the written tradition (even, ironically, as it marks a speech). However, when the formulaic language appears, ("when Mama got around to Henry Ford . . ." 23) the language moves further along the continuum towards the oral tradition. It is at this juncture that Mrs. MacTeer's language literally leaps off the page and disappears into the realm of orality, a realm which exists beyond the continuum on the page. This leap occurs when, after a brief summary of the formulaic language, Mrs. MacTeer's monologue ends abruptly. Only short fragments from Mrs. MacTeer's soliloquy are cited in this passage thereafter. Thus, there is a large void created, the missing pieces of Mrs. MacTeer's monologue, which occur only in the realm of orality. The leap between the written to the oral here appears to be a leap between two different realms. How does the existence of the iterative narrative shape this world of orality? I find Genette's analysis of Marcel Proust sheds light on this question. He writes that Proust's "novel is . . . a novel of controlled, imprisoned, and bewit-ched time" (118). Surely the merger of the iterative and singulative modes contributes to this bewitched time. The singulative mode exemplified by Mrs. MacTeer's diatribe on the milk marks the linear, particularized description of time and place. But when she begins to repeat herself and use formulaic language—and she does this off the page, she enters a kind of nonlinear time, an always already place of language. The merger of these modes mark the movement within the linear, particularized world of the written (the here and the now) and the "imprisoned, controlled" formulaic language, which seldom deviates in expression.

This analysis of form, which reveals the presence of orality in Mrs. MacTeer's monologue, illuminates the content, the development of character and plot. Once again, Pecola is alienated by language. This time, she bears the brunt of Mrs. MacTeer's anger.[15] She does not reply to Mrs. MacTeer aloud, or silently. Nor does Pecola have the narrative opportunity to tell the story of what happened to her. It is Claudia who records the conversation. Claudia is the one who shapes her mother's words. In addition, Claudia makes it apparent that she is familiar with her mother's habits of venting. This is knowledge which Pecola does not have access to. Why is this knowledge important? Because Claudia's knowledge of her mother's linguistic habits reflects intimacy bred of familiarity. As a visitor, Pecola cannot know that Mrs. MacTeer's diatribe is habitual and that it always ends with song, which, as Claudia tells us, is "sweet" (24). How does Pecola know that the diatribe is normal (habitual) and that she can look forward to the song? It is telling that at precisely the point when Mrs. MacTeer's language does make the transition from the particular (the singulative mode concerning Pecola) to the generic (the formulaic language concerning Henry Ford), the girls leave. While Mrs. MacTeer's daughters know that the cycle must play its course, Pecola disappears before the monologue can be come cyclical. She leaves before she can begin to see the structure of the diatribe. She leaves before she can hear the singing. She leaves before she can recognize her entry into a world marked by the familiar, the controlled, the bewitched and the intimate.

This world of language, which the MacTeer daughters recognize, is marked by unarticulated lessons on how to cope with life's struggles, lessons familiar and repetitive within the Black community, as Holloway observes:

> Language becomes a means of catharsis and, following an ancient ritual from field days, song becomes a signal for many things inexpressible by action direct or indirect . . . The [MacTeer] girls learn from their mother, learn of their Blackness and their femaleness by listening to these sung messages and understanding better how to cope. (40)

In the world of Mrs. MacTeer's repetitive fussing soliloquies are lessons for releasing pain through a ritualized and patterned language of speech and song. Pecola misses the lessons of Mrs. MacTeer, which as Holloway astutely discovers, are certainly patterned on the slave's use of songs to release unspoken but powerful feelings of despair and remorse. Such cultural strategies Blacks used for coping with their response to their place in the world, through spoken language, are unavailable to Pecola.[16]

The words which Pecola does bear witness to are the fights her parents have. One peculiarity of the Breedlove discourse is the narrative surrounding this linguistic event. The written words assume some of the qualities of the oral realm in order to serve as Pecola's voice, as she silently observes her parents yelling and fighting with one another. My analysis of this event begins with the narrative:

> Even from where Pecola lay, she could smell Holly's whiskey. The noises in the kitchen became louder and less hollow. There was direction and purpose in Mrs. Breedlove's movements that had nothing to do with the preparation of breakfast. This awareness, supported by ample evidence from the past, made Pecola tighten her stomach muscles and ration her breath. Cholly had come home drunk. Unfortunately he had been too drunk to quarrel, so the whole business would have to erupt this morning. (35)

The narrator begins by explaining Pecola's awareness of the oncoming fight. Pecola reads the signs and is aware of their meaning. She smells the alcohol, she hears Mrs. Breedlove's complaint in her movements, and she reacts by tightening her muscles. The narrator continues to describe Pecola's awareness, even though her name is not mentioned. The sentence, "there was direction and purpose in Mrs. Breedlove's movements that had nothing to do with the preparation of breakfast," easily makes room for the expression of the narrator's and Pecola's awareness of the predicament. The narrator's words continue to give expression to Pecola's thoughts. The words summarize her conclusions based on her feelings: there would have to be a fight because Cholly had come home drunk and her parents had not quarreled. The narrator's words speak for Pecola using a device Volishinov calls "indirect discourse." To paraphrase Volishinov, indirect discourse can occur when the narrator expresses the ideas of a character, without using the character's manner of speech. When this occurs, the narrator does not "hear whatever there is in that utterance that is without thematic significance" (130). The narrator transmits Pecola's ideas, but she is not quoted directly, nor is her manner of speech received in the body of the narration.

Why aren't Pecola's thoughts carried in her own syntax? The indirect discourse best expresses her passivity and silence at the same time that it reveals her thoughts. Thus writing does not convey speech in the usual manner, through quotation marks. When this occurs, speech is given a material body, and in this sense made to conform to the realm of the written. However, in this case, something unusual happens. Pecola's voice, expressed through the narrator, is not conveyed directly in the material body of writing itself; and to this extent, the narration (with Pecola's voice) belongs to the body of what we call orality. For the essence of orality, like the evidence of Pecola's voice here, is not a material written body.

The Breedlove arguments, like Pecola's voice in the narrative, belongs to both categories of the written and the spoken: they contain both entirely written representations of conversation and partially written representations. In the partially written representatives. In the partially written conversations lies the implied, suggested, spoken realm.

The first written argument between Mr. and Mrs. Breedlove is presented in full, from beginning to end. A second, only partially recounted, is connected to the main body of the fight. The two fights repeat one another; they are two particular examples of iterable events. I discuss the structure of repetition and why this structure is so important for readers to gain insight into the Breedlove discursive nightmare. The first fight is predicted upon the existence of a chain of events:

> Cholly had come home drunk. Unfortunately, he had been too drunk to quarrel, so the whole business would have to erupt this morning. Because it had not taken place imme-diately, the oncoming fight would lack spontaneity; it would be calculated, uninspired, and deadly. (35)

The logic of their occurrence is evident here. Whenever Cholly comes home drunk, an argument ensues. If the argument does not occur at night, it occurs in the morning; and, as a result of the delay, takes on an added element of calculation. Perhaps the fight is more calculated precisely because the Breedloves feel compelled to complete the ritual of fighting which accompa-nies the drunkenness, and it is the void created by the unfulfillment of this ritual which makes iterability (the calculation, the lack of creativity) impera-tive. What is certain, but unspoken, is a structure of feeling which yokes the words exchanged by the Breedloves during this fight. The narrative names some of these feelings.

The arguments provide feelings of relief from the tiresomeness of poverty and replace the feelings of deadness with a sense of grandeur (36). As well, Mrs. Breedlove feels alive and zestful during a fight. These feelings, along with the hatred and fear which accompany fights, comprise the spectrum of ritualized and routine ceremony; they comprise the aura of the words which charges the oral communication. In stark contrast to the gossip exchanged by Mrs. MacTeer and her friends: the extra linguistic meaning produced from such communica-tion reinforces feelings of separateness. The words the Breedloves exchange are spoken but never heard, and the intimacy which comes from being on the same communicative wavelength is never felt. An examination of the words exchanged reveals just such miscommunication:

> Mrs. Breedlove came swiftly into the room and stood at the foot of the bed where Cholly lay. "I need some coal in this house." Cholly did not move. "Hear me?" Mrs. Breedlove jabbed Cholly's foot . . . "Awwww, woman!" (35)

The pace in this conversation is delayed by Cholly's silence. In his silence there is no cooperative prompting, no enthusiasm for Mrs. Breedlove's words. Their words do not overlap, excitedly, signaling casualness of rapport and familiarity. It is the slow pace of the conversation which excites Mrs. Breedlove to physical violence, accompanied by her telling words, "Hear me."

So particular are these words that it is hard for the reader to believe that these words are, in their exact form, iterative. They take on the appearance of a singularity.

On the other hand, the structure of feeling drives and shapes the words and the pattern of the words, marking the event as iterative. The iterability of this event reveals the volumes of fights structured like this one, which are never represented on page, fights which readers can only imagine because they remain only in the realm of the spoken.

This is the case with another, partially recorded fight between the Breedloves recorded in the same chapter:

> Often she [Mrs. Breedlove] could be heard discoursing with Jesus about Cholly, pleading with Him to help her "strike the bastard down from his pea-knuckle of pride." And once when a drunken gesture catapulted Cholly into the redhot stove, she screamed, "Get him, Jesus! Get him." (37)

The words, "Get him, Jesus!" are from another fight. The complete details of this fight—why it started and what else was said and done are unknown, unwritten. Mrs. Breedlove's outburst is a particular example of the iterative structure of this fight. The structure here is evident in the first line of this passage: the fights often contain Mrs. Breedlove's discourse with Jesus. The addition of this small tale emphasizes the sheer impact of the Breedlove's exchange, because of its emphasis on predictability, timelessness, and receptiveness. Secondly, the tale increases the element of hopelessness which permeates each sentence of this chapter on the Breedloves. Mrs. Breedlove invokes the power of a divine force which epitomizes mercy and love of the purpose of revenge and damnation. She does so without recognizing that her own hands are unclean and her own soul is in need of a sea change (of redemption). Surely, her words, which are so repetitive that they are fossilized, reveal a state of mind long resistant to the kind of love and attention she so desperately fights for. In this sense perhaps the iterability itself "speaks" volumes about the Breedloves.

My analysis of the Breedloves' discourse introduces some unorthodox written representations of speech and voice, insofar as the written only partially represents what is spoken. I now turn my attention to an event in which the written represents what is unspoken. I begin this section with an analysis of what appears to be an excerpt from a Dick and Jane primer which is placed, suddenly, in the chapter on the Breedlove fights.

The excerpt from the primer is prefaced by the narrator's commentary on Pecola's reactions to her parents' fight. Pecola links her parents' behavior to the way they look. She muses that if she looked different, and her parents looked different, then they would not fight. Instead she muses, "Maybe they'd say, 'why, look at pretty-eyed Pecola. We mustn't do bad things in front of those pretty eyes" (40).[17] The Dick and Jane primer improvisation follows.

> Pretty eyes. Pretty blue eyes. Big blue pretty eyes. Run, Jip, run. Jip runs, Alice runs. Alice has blue eyes. Jerry has blue eyes. Jerry Runs. Alice runs. They run with their blue eyes. Four blue eyes. Four Pretty blue eyes. Blue-sky eyes. Blue-like Mrs. Forrest's blue blouse eyes. Morning-glory-blue-eyes. Alice-and-Jerry-blue-storybook eyes. Alice-and-Jerry-blue-story-book-eyes. (40)

In the passage which precedes the Dick and Jane primer excerpt, readers are informed of who speaks: Pecola imagines her parents speaking. The words they speak are marked with quotation marks. Even though this linguistic event is neither simple, nor straightforward—the quotation marks signify Pecola's thoughts—there is, at least, a modicum of signifying difference between this event and the Dick and Jane primer. The primer comes without introduction. Its words are attributed to none of the characters. There are no quotation marks. Furthermore, it appears to be a textual for several reasons. Its short, repetitive syntactical units contrast with those of the words which come before it. The names mentioned: Jerry, Alice, and Jip are stock names from a series of readers that competed with the Dick and Jane. And the simple, child-like glorification of appearance (blue eyes) and behavior (running) imitate stock phrases from the primers. In short, the primer assumes the function of a world which is separate from *The Bluest Eye*.

However separate the two passages may appear to be, they speak intertextually to one another. The Dick and Jane primer focuses on the blue eyes. The eyes are desirable because everyone, Jip, Alice, and Jerry, seems to have them. The repetition of the words "blue eyes" trumpets and reinforces their omnipresence. This fixation underlies Pecola's own fixation with blue eyes. Not only does the primer speak with *The Bluest Eye*, but it speaks for it. The words in the Dick and Jane primer belong to Pecola. The evidence for this lies in the passage which immediately follows it. The passage reads: "Every night, without fail, she prayed for blue eyes" (40). Perhaps the Dick and Jane primer is Pecola's prayer.

If it is true that in fact the passages cited above replicate the gestures of orality, then it is also true that several layers of irony operate within this text to negate these gestures. First, he words of the primer are not from a real primer. The last sentence in the excerpt exposes its falsity. The level of self-consciousness carried by the words, "Alice and Jerry blue storybook eyes," is not found in storybooks. Secondly, the presence of this self-conscious sentence imbues the entire passage with irony. If blue eyes are found in storybooks, then they are as elusive as storybook fantasies: they are not to be had by little Black girls in general and Pecola in particular. From this vantage point, the words of the primer do not "speak" (explicitly reveal) their ironic underpinnings.

To discover other layers of complexity concerning the way the primer signifies the unspeakable in this discursive event, I rely on M.M. Bakhtin's analysis of discourse in the novel. Bakhtin writes of the ability of language to adopt:

> . . . specific points of view on the world, forms for conceptualizing the world in words . . . As such they all may be juxtaposed to one another, mutually supplement one another, contradict one another . . . [These struggling languages] are all able to enter into the unitary plane of the novel, which can unite in itself paradic stylizations of generic languages, various forms of stylizations and illustrations of professional and period bound language. (292)

The words of the primer may be viewed as the embodiment of a particular ideological system. Not only is the Dick and Jane primer a fantasy, but it is a script of the racist belief system which privileges White looks over Black.[18] This belief system dominates the world of words and ideas, and it also seeps into the written word of the Dick and Jane primer and *The Bluest Eye*. However, in *The Bluest Eye*, on the "unitary plane" of the novel, it engages in a dialogue (and sometimes a heated argument) with the words and belief systems which dispute it. Parody, as Bakhtin notes, is used here to mark the war of words. I have mentioned one form of this parody, the way in which the primer announces its falsity. I would like to further analyze the war going on here by making use of Bakhtin's concept of "hybrid construction" to describe the way irony works in this passage.

Bakhtin writes that a hybrid construction is ". . . an utterance that belongs, by its grammatical (syntactic) and compositional markers, to a single speaker, but that actually contains mixed within two utterances, two speech manners . . . two axiological belief systems" (304). The grammar of the primer, as I discussed above marks it as a separate text syntactically from The Bluest Eye, and Pecola. As Bakhtin notes, there is hybrid construction—and, in fact, there is an additional voice here. In all, there are three voices. The words of the primer embody their own belief systems, and they also embody those of Pecola's. These are two of the voices: the distinct voice of the storybook, and the prayer Pecola utters. The third voice provides the irony. Pecola does not share this parodic, ironic voice because she has not acquired a conscious level of resistance to the ideology she espouses. In fact, her "prayer" finally emerges in her own words when she petitions the quack, Soaphead, for blue eyes; and he, in the guise of a false god, answers it (137).[19]

The third voice makes a mockery of Pecola's passive acceptance of these storybook words. It represents the growing social awareness, during the time these books were in use, of the effects of dominant ideology on the self-esteem of Blacks.[20] The presence of three voices results in a peculiar discursive relationship. The war of words actually takes place between the voice of irony and the voice of the primer; Pecola is excluded from actively participating in this war. Although readers may listen to the discursive battle fought on Pecola's behalf, Pecola does not; in this sense that battle remains unspoken. Pecola does not hear the (ironic) words which may heal her, just as she never hears the singing of Mrs. MacTeer, and she is excluded from the community of gossip (between Mrs. MacTeer and friends) which confers humanity.[21]

Although the Breedloves are ostracized from healing words, one member of the family, Pecola's father Cholly, has one—and only one—opportunity to receive words of healing. This event, like the last one described, also does not have any of the orthodox representations of the spoken word. It occurs when Cholly's caretaker, Aunt Mimmy, is sick and receives a visit from her friends. She is given medicine by M'Dear, the "competent midwife and decisive diagnostician" (108). The significance of her presence and that of other elders here is emphasized. M'Dear's powers are trumpeted by the narrator. She is the one who is called when ordinary means of healing fail. The other women laud her accomplishments and begin to weave them, along with Aunt Jimmy's condition, into a fabric of conversation about healing and sickness:

> Rising and falling, complex in harmony, uncertain in pitch, but constant in the recitative of pain. They hugged the memories of illnesses to their bosoms. They licked their

lips and clucked their tongues in fond rembrance of pains they had endured—childbirth, rheumatism, croup, sprains, backaches, piles. (109)

Not only do they recite their record illnesses, but they remember their survival of abuses at the hands of both Whites and Blacks. They talk about what it means to be black women who sustain families during hard times, and to reach old age having endured it all. They dwell on their survival, having reached the status where they were: ". . . old enough to be irritable when and where they chose, tired enough to look forward to death, disinterested enough to accept the idea of pain while ignoring the presence of pain . . . and at last, free" (110). This blessed status, achieved only at the expense of enduring and surviving hardships, is what enables Cholly to be comforted. It has this effect:

> The lullaby of grief enveloped him, rocked him, and at last numbed him. In his sleep the foul odor of an old woman's stools turned into the healthy smell of horse shit . . . He was aware in his sleep, of being curled up in a chair, his hands tucked between his thighs. In a dream his penis changed into a long hickory stick, and the hands caressing it were hands of M'Dear. (110)

Clearly, the conversation, which he does not hear on the conscious level (in the same way that Claudia does not hear her mother's gossip), seeps into his unconscious while he is sleeping. It allows him to sleep and calms his fears of his caretaker dying. The talk of survival convinces him that this illness, too, shall pass. He instinctively senses, through his powers of smell, that his aunt is healing; the smell of her stool changes miraculously. Since Aunt Jimmy is also sleeping, it may be that the conversation of the elders contributes to the healing power of the medicine M'Dear dispenses. The hickory stick (which M'Dear wields when she comes to see Aunt Jimmy) also appears in Cholly's dream. Why does Cholly dream of M'Dear stroking his hickory-stick penis? The conversation literally augments Cholly's manhood. The physical and communal healing (the talk of the women supporting their families) which takes place here also translates into a feeling of wellbeing and comfort needed to turn a boy like Cholly into a man.[22]

The healing word is, no doubt, invoked by the presence of what Morrison calls the "ancestor." She maintains that in Black fiction, the ancestor, who is benevolent, advising, wise and protective presides over and heals the city, country, or village in which she lives. And protagonists who do not have access to the ancestor are alienated.[23] The ancestor here is clearly M'Dear and the other elders. When Aunt Jimmy dies and Cholly wanders from the protective territory of his home, his sexuality is challenged and scarred by White who force him to have sex with his girlfriend. The humiliation Cholly feels is never healed by the ancestors. As a result, he tries to release feelings of emasculation when he fights with Mrs. Breedlove (37) and when he rapes his daughter, Pecola (127). In short, the importance of the healing aura which surrounds the spoken word in Cholly's life is immeasurable, as we see through the effects of its loss.

Heretofore, I have described the way the written word mimics the spoken, without conventional representations of conversation. In the first instance (concerning the Dick and Jane primer) the war of words on the page imitates the gestures of discourse, as Bakhtin points out in his analysis; and in so doing, the written word (which is associated with stasis) enjoys the play of the spoken word without ever changing its identity. In the second event (concerning Cholly and the elders) the written word describes precisely what it cannot do: send forth healing which lies in the sound—not in the sense—of the word. In both examples, the words enter the realm of unconscious thought. But the next linguistic example deals with the representation of conscious thought.

The chapter on Mrs. Breedlove (Pauline) uses a mixture of conventional and unconventional representations of the spoken word to signify its true identity as conscious, unspoken thought. Here is an example:

> "When I first seed Cholly, I want you to know it was like all of the bits of color from the time down home when all us chil'ren went berry picking after a funeral and I put some in the picket of my Sunday dress, and they mashed up and stained my hips . . ." (92)

Mrs. Breedlove's words are different from Mrs. MacTeer's in one important respect: hers are italicized. Italics are used to mark unusual linguistic events in this novel. They are used to mark the Dick and Jane primer excerpt quoted above (and in the text's preface) and they are used to mark Pecola's inner dialogue when she becomes insane.[24] The italics, then are used to represent the unspoken, and—more precisely—unconscious thought. These italics, however, are combined with quotation marks, which imply that the words are spoken.[25] This unusual combination of looks: quotation marks and italics are not to be found elsewhere in the book. Together, they symbolize that which can be spoken, but is not; they mark the space between what is spoken aloud and what is unspeakable.

Other textual clues support this hypothesis. Unlike Mrs. MacTeer's monologue, Mrs. Breedlove's speech occurs outside of a time and place. Nor does the omniscient narrator ever name the person to whom she is speaking. It is also uncertain whether her speech is a monologue or part of a conversation. Mrs. MacTeer's words, on the other hand, are given temporal and spatial context.

The narrator, her daughter Claudia, tells us where and when Mrs. MacTeer speaks; and her monologue is identified as such. Although Mrs. Breedlove's speech is never contextualized, it does appear as if she is having a conversation with someone intimate and familiar because she reveals intimate and familiar details about her life.

The fact that Mrs. Breedlove reveals a great deal of retrospective and an introspective thought to no one in particular lends weight to the argument that she is, in fact, just thinking. The particular style which characterizes Mrs. Breedlove's words serves the purpose of signifying (in yet another way) unspoken words which must be spoken. Mrs. Breedlove has no one to talk to; yet she must tell her story.

Oddly enough, the language Morrison uses for Mrs. Breedlove's thoughts falls into the category of oral Black English, given that Standard English is used to mark unconscious thought in italics elsewhere in the novel. Mrs. Breedlove's language is, to use Morrison's terms: and it relies "for full comprehension on codes embedded in black culture."[26] In this way, Mrs. Breedlove's thought is made to depend on representations of the spoken.

Also odd is the way in which Mrs. Breedlove's speech is heavily dependent upon the words of the omniscient narrator for clarity of voice. In other words, her thought is made to depend on the "writerly" (the epitome of the written word) narration for its expression. Here is what the narrator says before Mrs. Breedlove's passage. "He came, strutting right out of a Kentucky sun on the hottest day of the year. He came big, he came strong, he came with yellow eyes, flaring nostrils, and he came with his own music" (91). The narrator gives information which Pauline witholds, explaining when Cholly comes, where he comes from, and how he looks. By contrast, Pauline's focuses on how she feels when she first meets him. There is a classic distinction between Pauline's language and the narrator's. If Pauline's language adopts the form of orality (because it is speakerly and colloquial), then the narrator's standard English, and its tendency to be what critic David Olson calls "autonomous," marks it as writerly.

Autonomous language is more often found in written than in oral texts, and is associated with the essay form. According to Olson, the words are written in such a "manner that the sentence [is] an adequate, explicit representation of the meaning, relying on no implicit promises or personal interpretations" (268). In the above example, the narrator tends to provide the details which the speaking character omits. These details are necessary for the reader to fully comprehend Mrs. Breedlove's words. In so doing, the narrative allows

Mrs. Breedlove the freedom to assume the familiarity of a spoken, intimate style. As a result, readers can know Mrs. Breedlove intimately, while being aware of the fact that no one in her world knows her intimately. In this way, the words of the narrator and of Mrs. Breedlove in their various forms (writerly, speakerly, standard English, colloquial) work together to speak on Pauline's behalf.

In what way is the excerpt from Mrs. Breedlove's speech affected by the realm of the oral? There are several answers to this question because the written word is innovative and varied in this passage. Mrs. Breedlove's thoughts are informed by the rhetoric of orality, especially its colloquial sound and familiar expression. In this way, the written word mimics the style of the oral.

In the case of the narrator's voice, expressed in writerly style, the written does not assume the style or rhythm of the oral, but rather, it protects its appearance as the "essence" of writing, in so far as this essence is associated with autonomous language.[27]

At the same time, the writerly expression of the narrator also serves the function of enhancing the orality of Mrs. Breedlove's written language. Conversely, the orality of Mrs. Breedlove's written language enhances the writerly expression of the narrator's voice. This is achieved because Morrison places Mrs. Breedlove's colloquial expression in sharp relief against the narrator's writerly expression. This achievement calls to mind, at first glance, the presence of binary opposite traditions of the spoken and the written—even as it reinforces, at second glance, the chameleon nature of the written word and its ability to define and suggest the spoken event when it exists in its most writerly form. The narrator's words, which may be regarded as the essence of writing—and the source which is least likely to have anything in common with the oral realm, has a hidden agenda: it shares the **goals** of the oral realm, which is to create after its own kind, when it inadvertently enhances the orality of Mrs. Breedlove's words. Where this peculiar juxtaposition occurs in the narrative, it may be said that the continuum between the oral and the written is evident.

I begin the analysis of the last linguistic event in this chapter, Pecola's mad speech,[28] by comparing the ways in which Pecola's speech is anticipated by Mrs. Breedlove's. Mrs. Breedlove's conversation represents the fullest expression of unspoken thought represented in the guise of the spoken word analyzed so far. Mrs. Breedlove's words anticipate Pecola's in the sense that both are represented as conversations, but in actuality, are dialogues held in the mind. In the case of Mrs. Breedlove, the dialogue is held between herself and the narrator, who hears her thoughts and reports them to the readers. The narrator opens the door to her thoughts, and places them in context. The linguistic event of Pecola's madness carries the concept of dialogue a bit further (in the sense that the conversation shows Pecola talking directly to her imaginary friend), but the narrator's role is diminished, and as a result, readers are thrown, unprepared, far more deeply into Pecola's thought than Mrs. Breedlove's.

Unlike the words of her mother, Pecola's mad conversation is not prefaced by the narrator; Pecola's imagined dialogue opens the beginning of the chapter. Nor does the narration interrupt the conversation with explanatory remarks, as was the case with Mrs. Breedlove. Only at the end of Pecola's conversation does the narrator comment, vaguely, about its contents. The point here is that Morrison turns up the volume of the unspeakable and unspoken by diminishing the preparatory material (writerly narrative), explanatory devices (quotation marks), and substitutional fabric (hidden dialogue) which accompany representations of unspoken thought elsewhere in The Bluest Eye. When these markers are missing, what becomes apparent is Pecola's fullest explicit expression of her thought, her voice. As a result, readers are given more immediate access to the recesses of this character's mind.

Heretofore, I have examined unspoken words which never enter the realm of the written word on the page (as in the case of Mrs. MacTeer's monologue, the fight of the Breedloves, Mrs. MacTeer's gossip, and the conversation of the elders). In addition, I examined unconscious thought which enters the written word of the narrator (such as the Breedlove fight), or which expresses itself intertextually (such as the Dick and Jane). Each of these events can be regarded as forming a kind of pattern in which unspoken thought comes closer to being expressed openly. The expression of this revelation takes the guise of a spoken word. This is why Mrs. Breedloves' and Pecola's thoughts, at the end of the chapter, explicitly reveal the inner thoughts as dialogue, rather than being hidden in the narrative.

In the next two chapters, I will analyze the language of Beloved, examining the way in which the experiments in The Bluest Eye anticipate unspeakable and unspoken language written almost two decades later.

· 3 ·

WRITING AND SPEAKING FOR THE OTHER: THE FORMATION OF THE LINGUISTIC BODY OF THE SLAVE NARRATIVES AND *BELOVED*

For I have given unto them the words which thou hast given me
John 17:8

In this scripture lies the organizing concept of my argument in this chapter, which is best illustrated in the figure of speech (and I mean this literally) suggested by Christ's words. In John 17:8 Jesus speaks to God, announcing the accomplishment of his mission: he has given his disciples the words God has given him. In this figure three bodies are connected: the Father, the Son, and the disciples of

God. Through language, Christ gives his disciples the authority to speak for God—to be used as the vehicle through which God's Word is spoken. Thus, His disciples write the authentic spoken word of the Lord in the Bible. What occurs in this figure is the transference of the Word from the self to the other in such a way as to enable the other to write/speak for the self. The purity and power and truth of the word are retained even in its translation through space and time; boundaries of the self and the other; material word and material body; and the written and spoken. Yet, richly and strangely, the identity of these discreet entities is also maintained.

The idea that the self can speak and write for the other and still maintain its (self and the other's) identity is the specific behavior of language in the Word which becomes the ideal symbol for the **acts** of language in *Beloved*.

This symbol represents two of Morrison's rhetorical maneuvers. The first concerns her stated goals and intentions in her essay "The Site of Memory" with respect to her novel *Beloved*. In this essay, she describes how she gains access to a "kind of truth" about slavery, using her memory and imagination; and she produces this truth in her fiction (112). Thus, Morrison authenticates the means by which she gains access to the truth through her memory to produce her novel. Her authenticating strategy involves blurring the boundaries between fact and fiction, memory and imagination; in so doing, she validates as truth (a kind of truth) the fiction she has produced in her novel. Her essay is an authenticating document, which claims that her novel can speak (write) the truth about slavery.

If we take Morrison's claims seriously, we realize that her document of authentication also answers the questions of authenticity leveled at the slaves' narratives. How can we be certain that the slave narratives are authentic? Can we be sure that White abolitionists did not indeed influence (or author) the language of the slave? How can we be sure the narratives reveal the entire truth? Would not their words have been designed to appease white audiences? Indeed, the criticism of these narratives has consistently raised these questions. These questions are legitimized by the language of the slave narratives, which, through content and form, suggest—sometimes explicitly—the limitations of what they cannot say and their lack of control over what they do say, leaving (and perhaps leading) the audience to question the authenticity of the written word to speak for the experience of the slave.

"The Site of Memory" responds to such questions of authentication by insisting on the fusion of truth, fiction, and memory. It answers those who attacked slave narrators for failing to distinguish between memory, fact, and imagination. At some level, a degree of faith from audiences is required to believe that the slave narratives or the Bible contain truth (or a kind of truth). Those who believe that these documents (either the narratives or the Bible or both) are true cannot, in the final analysis, rely upon other material objects to justify their belief. This is why I think Morrison's essay leads us to question the distinction between epistemology and ontology. Faith in fiction (or even "fact") is confirmed at some point by our own being.

Morrison's second rhetorical maneuver which is best represented by the image of Christ speaking for the other lies in the construction of the form and content of *Beloved* itself. She produces a narrative form which speaks for the inner thoughts of the slave characters. The narrative bears much of the burden for communicating these thoughts because these characters do not relate them to others.

Such an **act** of language constitutes part of Morrison's response to the veiled language of the slave narrative itself, which often reveals implicitly and explicitly its inability to speak for the intimate thoughts of the slaves. Thus, Morrison moves the unspeakable and unspoken aspects of the written Black language of the slave narrative to a different level of representation; and in the process she inaugurates the creation of a form of written Black language which *can* speak for (more of) the psychological core of the slave.

In the process of creating a suitable receptacle of language which transforms and releases the slave's word, Morrison advances her own form of the unspeakable and unspoken, a form of language developed first in *The Bluest Eye* and discussed in my last chapter. We find in the narration of *Beloved* that the unspoken thoughts of the characters are given fuller expression and greater control of the narrative than in *The Bluest Eye*. In fact, whereas these unspoken thoughts were structured by the explanatory fabric of the narrative (as in the case of Pauline's words, and to a lesser degree, Pecola's words) in *The Bluest Eye*, in *Beloved*, the unspoken thoughts noticeably determine the structure of the narrative and are more fully released from the structure of the narrative at the apex of this story.

In *Beloved*, the form is imitated by the content: its theme is the quest for the release and reception of the slave's word. This is the mission of Sethe, the protagonist. My essay describes how she searches for an audience who will listen to her. She finds such an audience in Beloved and Denver, who speak for her (symbolically and literally).

I begin by analyzing the slave narratives in general, drawing on the texts of Harriet Jacobs and Frederick Douglass specifically. I discuss the way in which these texts respond to audiences who doubt(ed) their authenticity with language that suggests volumes unspeakable and unspoken. Specifically, I focus on the way in which Jacobs and Douglass reveal and curtail details of their memory. Then, I trace Morrison's response to these narratives in *Beloved*. Part of her response involves the way in which *Beloved* takes as its central theme the revelation of memories which have been unspoken. Another part of the response is the production of the unspeakable unspoken language discussed above. My goal here is not only to present new interpretations of the role of language in Douglass and Jacobs, but to place the elements of narration and language in *Beloved* within the framework of the African American tradition of letters.

The volumes unspeakable and unspoken by the slave to which Morrison responds are, of course, accompanied by the volumes spoken and written by slaves about their condition. Slaves managed to create a new American liter-ature, which impressed the experiences of their unique condition upon the Western literary tradition. The literature of these slaves functioned as the voice which recorded the oppression of slavery and the resistance of Blacks to their condition. And the production of this genre of letters was achieved despite tremendous odds and heavy duress; in fact, Blacks were forbidden by law to write, and they were rarely educated or even considered educable.[1]

It is the unspeakable and unspoken, however, with which Morrison's *Beloved* is especially concerned: Morrison's language responds to—and even recalls—that which could not have ever been recorded by the slave in writing. The evidence of what was never written in the slave narratives is a matter often revealed explicitly by the slaves themselves in their narratives, and discussed by literary scholars. Critics such as James Olney and William Andrews have documented the link between the repression of memory, the omission of what the slave witnessed as evidenced by the noticeable gaps in the narrative, and the threadbare details which often surround some testimonies, with the influence of their audiences upon their writing.

I select passages from Frederick Douglass's 1845 *Narrative of the Life of Frederick Douglass* and Harriet Jacobs' 1861 *Incidents in the Life of a Slave Girl* which illustrate such repression. The work of Douglass and Jacobs (who used the alias Linda Brent and will henceforth be referred to by that name) is used here to illustrate the way in which writing for the other (a hostile audience) forced them to diminish what they saw—(their Eye) and who they were (their I).[2] Each of the passages in these narratives have gaps in which memory (recorded in language) was omitted or slanted. Douglass and Brent bare the scars of repressed memory and bear the limitations of words differently. While the passage cited from Douglass's *Narrative* refuses to reveal the omission of any memory, the passage from Brent's *Incidents* explicitly admits this omission. I begin with Douglass's narrative.

The gaps in the passage from the *Narrative*, which describe Douglass's relationship to his mother are, as I said above, not evident in this text. One can only discern a gap in the *Narrative* when comparing this passage to the passage from Douglass's second autobiography, *My Bondage and My Freedom*, published ten years later.[3] Douglass explains in the *Narrative* that he saw his mother only a few times in his life, due to the common practice of separating the slave mother from the child when the child reaches its twelfth month. His short narration (less than a page) of their relationship ends with this bleak comment:

> Never having enjoyed, to any considerable extent, her soothing presence, her tender and watchful care, I received the tidings of her death with much the same emotions I should have probably felt at the death of stranger. (16)

In an astonishing elaboration upon the events told in the *Narrative*, Douglass expands upon his relationship with his mother and his feelings about her in *My Bondage*. In this second autobiography, a record which emphasizes his mother's care, protection, and legacy is detailed in a six page chapter entitled, "The Author's Parentage." In his revision of the account given in the *Narrative*, Douglass remembers an occasion which stood out among his encounters with his mother, which, as a rule, were short and few. He remembers feeling hungry after the mean plantation cook refused to feed him. He steals a few grains of corn to stave off the hunger and is surprised by the sudden appearance of his mother. What follows next—and the loving, poignant language that describes it—is repeated here:

> She took the corn from me, and gave me a large ginger cake, in its stead, she read Aunt Katy [the cook] a lecture which she never forgot. . . .That night I learned the fact, that I was not only a child, but *somebody's* child. The sweet cake my mother gave me was in the shape of a heart. . . . (emphasis his, 154–155)

This revelation is followed by his admission that "the side view of her face is imaged on my memory, and I take few steps in life, without feeling her presence; but the image is mute" (155). Yet, at the end of still more revealing disclosures of and tributes to her memory,[4] Douglass does not retract his original statement, made in the *Narrative*, concerning his estrangement from her. In fact, he repeats adamantly—and insists that the reader refrains from censoring him— that "I received the tidings of her death with no strong emotions for her, and with very little regret . . ." (157). What is the difference between the account of his mother given in the narrative and the autobiography? The difference does not lie in a contradiction of the facts, but in the arrangement of the facts. In the narrative, the facts are merely presented, but in the second account, the facts are placed in a symbolic universe. Ernst Cassirer defines the symbolic universe, as follows: "man does not live in a world of hard facts . . . he lives rather in the midst of imaginary emotions, in hopes and fears, in illusions and disillusions, in his fantasies and dreams" (25). In his second recollection, the substance of the cold fact that Douglass received the tidings of his mother's death with little emotion is complicated—rather than negated—by the recollection of non facts, remnants of the image of his mother, her intangible presence, the feelings he had when he saw her on one occasion, and the pride he now feels concerning his parentage and her maternal instincts. All of these impressions contribute to the presentation of a mother who is somehow larger than life in his imagination, even if she is not present in the material realm of cold, hard, facts.

Critic James Olney uses Cassirer's observations of the symbolic universe to discern the reason why so many of the slave narratives simply recorded the facts, while excluding the symbolic realm of these facts. The language of the slave narratives such as those written by William Wells Brown and Henry Bibb were limited in the sense that they did not, for the most part, contain memory, or what Cassirer calls, "symbolic memory." Symbolic memory, simply put, is the experience of the cold hard facts, plus one's imaginative reconstruction of them.[5] Olney determines that the reason why many slave narratives refrained from this kind of memory is because their audiences would have distrusted their accounts:

> To give a true picture of slavery as it really is, he must maintain that he exercises a clear-glass, neutral memory that is neither creative nor faulty—indeed, if it were creative it would be . . . understood by skeptical readers as a synonym for lying. (150)

Indeed, as Douglass admits himself, he was directed by abolitionists to refrain from the realm of the imagination, limiting him to the facts, an order which he followed: " 'Let us have the facts,' said the people. So also said Friend George Foster who always wished to pin me down to my simple narrative" (367). Douglass's resistance to this simplicity is registered in My Bondage, where, as critic Peter Dorsey contends, Douglass complicates and reshapes some of the literary conventions which influenced slave narratives in general, and the Narrative in particular. Dorsey argues that the Narrative was especially tailored for the Christian antebellum audience, and used binary logic modeled on Christian conversion discourse. In My Bondage, says Dorsey, "he qualified, muted, or suppressed the language of conversion with its sudden and radical reversals of binary terms" (438).

In the *Narrative's* description of Douglass's mother, the description of his relationship with his mother relies on binary distinctions such as presence and absence; and life and death. However, *My Bondage* erases such distinctions. For example, it records the image of his mother's face, an image which is ever present and speaks volumes of her love and commitment—even if "mute" (unspoken), and which inhabits the murky realm of feelings and imagination instead of neutral facts. Such an image becomes, in Douglass's hands, a metaphor both for the untimely death of his mother, who died a slave, and the resilience of his mother's presence, which, even after death, confers pride and maternal love upon him. Douglass reconfigures the realm of truth-as-fact, determined to include the imagination in order to locate his parentage and to release and convey the stories of his memory.[6]

Whereas Douglass's *Narrative* affirms the factual details of his memory but negates the symbolic configuration of his memory, Brent's *Incidents* negates the factual details, but affirms the symbolic configuration of her memory. Brent uses figurative language to articulate her symbolic memory, her configuration of a series of events, and her hopes and fears pertaining to these events. This configuration of events is only suggested figuratively: Brent refuses to disclose the traumatic factual details.

Metaphor and metonymy are the vehicles Brent uses to describe repeated sexual abuse which she suffered at the hands of her master, Dr. Flint. The passage which follows narrates the beginning of these incidents:

> But I now entered on my fifteenth year—a sad epoch in the life of a slave girl. My master began to whisper foul words in my ear . . . He tried his utmost to corrupt the pure principles my grandmother had instilled. He peopled my young mind with unclean images, such as only a vile monster could think of. (27)

When read quite literally, the exchange between Brent and her master occurs only through language, foul language. However, when the use of metaphor and metonymy are analyzed closely, the images described here suggest physical violation. M.H. Abrams provides useful definitions of these terms. Both terms suggest the figurative substitution for a literal term. But there is a key distinction between them. In metaphor, such a substitution occurs "without asserting a comparison" between the literal and figurative expressions (67). In metonymy, the substitution occurs between terms which are closely associated "because of contiguity in common experience" (69).

Barbara Johnson's analysis of metaphor and metonymy found in Zora Neale Hurston's *Their Eyes Were Watching God* can be useful in relation to Brent's passage to produce Brent's configuration of her victimization at the hands of Dr. Flint. Johnson says:

> Here we find an internalization of the outer: Janie's inner self resembles a store. The material for this metaphor is drawn from the narrative world of contiguity: the store is the place where Joe has set himself up as lord. (163)

Johnson finds a relationship between Janie's inner self and her outer surroundings in the narrative. Her inner self is compared metaphorically to a store. Hurston constructs a metonymical relationship between the store of the inner self which resembles the contiguous settings of the store on the outside of her self (163).

Likewise, Brent also makes a distinction between the inner and the outer self. In the passage cited above, her narrative begins with what happens outside of her body before narrating the events inside the body, which are related metaphorically and metonymically to the outside. She begins her story by mentioning the time when these events occurred, a time which is a "sad epoch in the life of a slave girl" (27). This time is important because it marks the age of puberty and the onslaught of physical changes which occur in the bodies of young women during this time.

Brent makes it implicitly clear that many young slave women, and not just her, face sexual assault during this time. Brent makes this suggestion, however, without ever mentioning the word "rape." Still, she adds more details to the narrative, lest her meaning is lost. She observes that her master began to "whisper foul words in her ear" in an attempt to "corrupt the pure principles" (here chastity and virginity come to mind) her grandmother had taught her. Brent lets readers know that the master violates her mind with language. Surely this act is a kind of intangible penetration of the body (the brain and the ear).

This outer image is a surface and superficial representation of what really occurs on the outside. The image of what happens appears in the last sentence quoted in Brent's passage, which is an interiorization of the exterior self: "He peopled my young mind with unclean images, such as only a vile monster could think of" (27). The metaphor of the image as a person penetrating the inside of her mind, I suggest, is contiguously and metonymically related to what is never actually described on the outside: her body, forcibly "peopled" by her unclean master.

Brent uses metaphor and metonymy as the vehicles through which she breaks her silence and in so doing gains a kind of power through language which comes from her ability to both define and communicate her experience. Johnson's description of Hurston is aptly applied here:

> On the one hand, this means she knew how to keep the inside and the outside separate without trying to blend or merge them into one unified identity. On the other hand it means she has stepped irrevocably into the necessity of figurative language, where inside and outside are never the same. (163)

By reducing Dr. Flint's physical violation into a euphemistic image, Brent makes a psychological adjustment in her memory of what happened. She diminishes the experience to something which occurs figuratively in the regions of her mind. At the same time, she manages to communicate the total story, the complete symbolic configuration of what happened to her audiences, without explicitly relating the embarrassing details.

At the same time, I hasten to add, as Johnson does about Hurston's character Janie, that as a result of Brent's manipulation of metaphor and metonymy, she gains the capacity to articulate her own voice. Brent has certainly acquired a voice through figurative language, but it comes, paradoxically, at the cost of being dependent upon figurative language to tell a story which she cannot dare to remember in terms both literal and brutal. Her repression of literal memory is most assuredly linked to the outstanding pressures of her audiences' expectations.

As Hazel Carby argues, Brent's narrative addresses the ideological expectations that true women were chaste, pure, submissive, and pious. Brent's confessions concerning her sexuality threatened her reputation. Carby observes that her sexuality "was compromised in the very decision to print her story and gain her public voice" (49). Indeed, even her White editor, Maria Child, as Carby suggests, was not free from the stigma of being associated with Brent (49). In the preface to *Incidents*, Child acknowledges this stigma: "I am well aware that many will accuse me of indecorum for presenting these pages to the public" (2). The differences between the reality of sexual abuse in slavery and contemporary literary conventions for depictions of nineteenth century women are rofound. And in fact, Brent's account of her abuse was the first of its kind. Jean Yellin argues that *Incidents* is the only slave narrative that "takes as its subject the sexual exploitation of female slaves" (263).

Because there were no literary conventions concerning sexuality, audiences were likely to assume that her revelation could be considered fiction. As if to rebut these assumptions, Brent writes: "The degradation, the wrongs, the vices, that grow out of slavery, are more than I can describe. They are greater than you would willingly believe" (28). Although she responds to her audience's distrust explicitly in this direct address, she also responds to her audience's distrust implicitly in the shape of her narrative structure. Ironically, Brent depends upon the common tools of fiction, metaphor and metonymy, in order to avoid the appearance of fiction and the discovery of the facts in the narrative.

Brent's use of language in her narrative is representative of a wide body of slave narratives, which, to paraphrase William Andrews, explored indirectly through metaphor what could not be explicitly divulged. Andrews argues that the late eighteenth and early nineteenth century slave narratives written by Black religious autobiographers invited metaphorical comparisons between spiritual pilgrims and themselves. In so doing, as Andrews points out, "there is a spiritual identity between Mr. Christian [the character who seeks God in John Bunyan's *Pilgrim's Progress*] and the [Black] narrator as pilgrims that makes it possible to accept the one as an attribute of the other" (11). Thus, the narratives challenged implicitly the belief that the presence of essential racial qualities meant that Blacks could not be spiritually (and therefore materially) equal to Whites. The location of this challenge in a metaphor rather than in bold—or even hostile— language made plain, was no doubt intended to prevent the alienation of White Christian readers.

What the passages from Brent and Douglass show,[7] is that the reduction of memory—in its form as both strictly fact and symbolic imagination—must be regarded as the result of writing for the other rather than the self. The other constitutes the real and localized audiences who, in Douglass's case, demanded just the facts; or in the case of Brent, the imagined, generalized audiences who subscribed to dominating ideals. Of course, these audiences were not mutually exclusive: each author would have been subjected to the pressures of audiences both real and imagined. Whether or not the writing of Douglass and Brent was self censored or self conscious, these are the results: the censorship of their memory and the reduction of what is seen (the eye) and what is experienced (the I), constitute the language which is emblematic of what is unspoken by the slave. Such language, then, is the production of a fiction, because it falls short of the truth in its attempt to represent a fiction audiences would accept as the truth.

In her essay, "The Site of Memory," Toni Morrison responds as a reader to this quandary of language:

> Over and over, the writers pull the narratives up short with such a phrase as, "But let us drop a veil over   these proceedings too terrible to relate." In shaping the experi- ence to make it palatable to those who were in a position to alleviate it, they were silent about many things, and they "forgot" many other things. (110)

Here, Morrison bemoans her access to what really happened; she expresses a wish to understand their identity (their I) and what they saw (their eyes). Furthermore, she makes the connections between silence and memory, and audience and narrative. She discovers how writing for the other can diminish the self. If she could not, as a reader, penetrate this realm of language, buffeted by a narrative designed to veil, then how could she as a writer communicate the experience of the slave through language?

The strategy she uses to rip the veil of language employed in the slave narrative is also divulged in her essay. After announcing that she uses her own recollections and the recollections of others, as well as the act of imagination to reconstruct the past, she describes the process this entails:

> It's a kind of literary archeology: on the basis of some information and a little bit of guesswork you journey to a site to see what remains were left behind and reconstruct the world that these remains imply. What makes it fiction is the nature of the imaginative act: my reliance on the image—on the remains—in addition to recollection, to yield up a kind of a truth. By "image," of course, I don't mean "symbol"; I simply mean "picture" and the feelings that accompany the picture. (111–112)

A fundamental shift is made in this passage between the truth documented in the written word and the truth accessed and validated through one's own body. Unlike the audiences (past and present) which read and distrust the presentation of truth in the slaves' written words, Morrison does not rely solely on material evidence to yield the truth. Instead, she privileges a system of intangible unspoken images of the past which are readily produced through her own body. These images are both located within the body of her imagination and memory, which are always already connected to the imagination and memories of others.[8]

In addition, the images are produced when she visits the sites of the material evidence: they constitute the pictures which come into her mind when she holds an artifact produced by a slave (such as a slave narrative); thus memories exist outside of the body and occupy sites. Surely Douglass's image of his mother, which continually abides in his memory, is the kind of image Morrison describes; such an image transcends place and time and is the means by which a self witnesses to the other. From the body of the slave emanates the unspoken image, the authentic record of what transpired; this image is received by another body which shares this image. Such communication knows no boundaries between the self and the other—even as those boundaries remain distinct.

In discovering and revealing and authenticating this paradigm, Morrison necessarily deconstructs the binary opposites of self and other, writer and reader, and truth and fiction, memory and imagination, epistemology and ontology. Because of the existence of binary thinking, audiences were reluctant to listen to the stories slaves had to tell. Audiences privileged memory over imagination, and truth over fiction; thus they determined that the existence of what they thought was imagination and fiction in the narratives was untrustworthy. Audiences trusted their ways of knowing the truth (through the existence of what they determined to be facts); thus they never allowed a way of knowing which could be produced through one's own being. Audiences never imagined that a bridge of language (let alone mute images such as the one in *Bondage*) could allow the boundaries between the self and the other to blur in order to create a shared experience; thus the audiences determined and influenced a writing which could only be written for the other.

In addition to creating that part of language in the slave narrative which was veiled, the existence of binary thinking among audiences determined to imprison the memory of the slaves indefinitely. Writers who sought to release the memories of the slaves in a narrative would always, under the paradigm of binary thinking be subject to the same restrictions. Under the system of binary thinking, any language which sought to release those memories would be determined to be fiction.

This is why Morrison necessarily fudges the boundaries between these binary opposites:

> Therefore the crucial distinction for me is not the difference between fact and fiction, but the distinction between fact and truth. Because facts can exist without human intelligence, but truth cannot. So if I'm looking to find and expose a truth [about the slaves] . . . then the approach that's most productive and most trustworthy for me is the recollection that moves from image to the text. Not from the text to the image. (113)

The binary opposite terms fact and fiction are no longer productive tools for discerning the truth about the past. Morrison acknowledges here the role of symbolic memory and factual memory. The symbolic memory is the fiction necessary to construct the truth. And such fiction involves memory. Writing the truth involves producing language from the unspoken images located in the memory—not producing images created purely from the language (without the aid of such images).

Thus, Morrison authenticates the means by which she gained access to the truth through memory to produce her novel *Beloved*. In other words, by blurring the boundaries between fact and fiction; self and other; and memory and imagination, she validates as truth the fiction she has produced in her novel. The truth about Margaret Garner (the slave on whose story Morrison's novel is based) can therefore be communicated in *Beloved*, even though Morrison based much of the novel upon her imagination, rather than from fragments of the story located in a newspaper.[9]

Beloved, then, is a slave narrative which communicates the truth ("a kind of truth") about its subjects. But not only does Morrison succeed in authenticating her own novel, but she rebukes—once and for all—the denigration of that which is fiction in the slave narratives. This is why I call Morrison's essay, "The Site of Memory," an authenticating document—the last authenticating document. The original documents of authentication, as Robert Stepto reminds us, were documents written by slave holders and abolitionists that were attached to the slave narratives to authenticate the former slave's account. Both Douglass and Brent had such documents attached to their narratives; the voices of the abolitionists attested to the veracity of their stories. Indeed, so ubiquitous is the presence of these authenticating documents among the narratives, that they must, in fact, be regarded as part and parcel of the slave narrative genre—and therefore, part of the language of distrust and disempowerment emanating from the narratives.[10] As Stepto argues, the authenticity of these slaves as narrators was diminished by the presence of these authenticating documents, which, by their very existence, undermined their authorship and validated the impulses of audiences to question the authenticity of their narratives.

Morrison's authenticating document differs from these original documents in several ways. First, it is not attached to her novel. In addition, it does not claim that the events in *Beloved* are factual—although it does claim that it tells the truth because of its special reliance on memory and fiction. Thirdly, it is written by Morrison herself, as opposed to being written by a slaveholder, an abolitionist, or a scholar. And finally, to repeat what I said earlier, it validates fiction as a means to tell a valid and authentic story. This is why she begins her essay by discussing the "authenticity" of her presence as a fiction writer in a discourse on autobiography and memoir. She argues that "the authenticity of my presence here [in the discourse on autobiography] lies in the fact that a very large part of my own literary heritage is the autobiography" (103). In this rhetorical move, she links fact and fiction. The "factual" in the slave narrative gives birth to her "fiction." The authenticity of her fiction to speak for the narratives comes from the body of language which we call African American literature. This body expresses a line of continuity between past and present, fact and fiction.

An examination of this body of African American letters reveals that Morrison's authenticating document has precedence among twentieth century writers.[11] Barbara Foley notes the existence of a category of such writers who, to paraphrase her words, strengthened the claims of their fiction to truth by appending documentary evidence (394). Richard Wright wrote prefaces to *Native Son* and *Uncle Tom's Children* which made claims for the typicality and validity of the characters of these novels among Blacks in the real world. Margaret Walker's *Jubilee*, which combines fact and fiction also has an authenticating document, which appears in a separate publication. In *How I Wrote Jubilee*, Walker details her method by which she collected data about her ancestors, who are the subject of her novel. More broadly, the claim for authenticity and truth which Morrison has made for *Beloved* is the same claim made by literature which Foley groups in the category she calls "the documentary mode of Black literature." In this mode the literature combines fact and fiction to produce a discourse which represents Black history. Foley argues, "part of this insistence on a strong factual presence in Afro-American literature is an inevitable reaction against the disbelief of a predominantly white audience . . ." (391). Within this category of the documentary form, Foley has noted the presence of subcategories, in which variations of mixture of fact and fiction can be found. While it is not the purpose of this essay to review all of these categories, it is fitting to mention some of the authors (in addition to the ones mentioned above) whom Foley has placed within the broad category of the documentary mode. She includes all of the slave narratives within this mode. In the twentieth century, she includes such authors as John Williams, Alex Haley, Ernest Gaines, Ralph Ellison, and Ishmael Reed.[12] Again, what distinguishes Morrison's work from these works of fiction is her especially strong emphasis, through her authenticating document, on the necessity of fiction to reveal (unspoken) truth and to unleash memory.

Establishing an emphasis on and necessity for the fiction in her fiction to release the truth is only part of what distinguishes Morrison from other Black writers. A close textual analysis of key passages in *Beloved* reveals that Morrison's goal is nothing short of shaping a language which releases memory (hers and the slaves) from many of the constraints imposed upon it by the expectations and influences of audiences past and present.

To accomplish this goal, Morrison reconceptualizes the relationship between narration, audience, and memory. In the original relationship manifested in the slave narratives, the narrator often pulls short, refusing to reveal all of his/her memories so that he/she will not offend his audiences or depart from their expectations. In her reconceptualization in *Beloved*, two separate events reverse this relationship. In the first event, the omniscient narrator becomes the audience, the perfect audience. It is perfect in the sense that it receives and releases the authentic unspoken memories of the characters: and in this sense it sees through the eyes and witnesses (or becomes) the very identity (the I) of the characters. The omniscient narrator is the depository for the unspoken memories of the characters—revealing what the characters themselves cannot say to each other.[13] In the second event, which occurs later in the novel, some of the characters themselves become the perfect audiences for each other; and they each receive the unspoken memories from each other.

What separates and determines this sea change of form (narration) are the quiet but seismic changes in the content. *Beloved* tells the story of the slave who desperately needs to remember and relate her story. Until she is able to find an audience, the narrator serves to release pieces of the story for her; the omniscient narrator serves as the blessed soul who, like Morrison herself, listens to untold memories. The shift in narration occurs when Sethe finally finds—after a long and fruitless search—the perfect audience who replicates and replaces the omniscient narrator until her story is told.

Beloved begins with Sethe's frustration, the result of years of pent-up anguish. Sethe does not want to remember how she murdered her own child during slavery, but the memories persist, and they are tangible. Thus, the novel begins with the haunting of Sethe's house by her dead baby girl. At first Sethe and her daughter Denver resist this haunting, then they succumb to it:

> So Sethe and Denver did what they could, and what the house permitted . . . Together they waged a perfunctory battle against the outrageous behavior of that place; against turned-over slop jars, smacks on the behind, and gusts of sour air. . . . Sethe and Denver decided to end the persecution by calling forth the ghost that tried them so. Perhaps a conversation, they thought, an exchange of views or something would help. So they held hands and said, "Come on. . . ." (4)

What Sethe realizes is that only a conversation with (and about) her past can save her. As she explains to Denver, the baby is angry because it has not heard Sethe's story about what happened—in a sense it has not been remembered, its death has not been explained. Sethe tells her daughter Denver that if the baby came, then "I could make it clear to her" (4). On one level, then, the house is Sethe's interior exteriorized. It is a metaphor for the battles she fought to suppress the past; and she recognizes that the only way to come to terms with the past is to tell it. Linda Brent's own desperate need to tell the story comes to my mind when I read Sethe's. When Dr. Flint abuses her, she "longed for some one to confide in. I would have given the world to have laid my head on my grandmother's faithful bosom, and told her all my troubles. . . ." (28).

Unlike this passage from Brent, Morrison's story does not simply operate on the symbolic level of memory, using symbolic language to suggest what is never quite made explicit. This is why the haunting of Sethe's house is also quite literal. The gusts of sour air and the smacks on the behind are real events. The calling forth of the baby does involve the literal communication with the dead. In *Beloved*, memories are tangible; they live and they overwhelm the senses. Rhetorically, Morrison's rendition of larger than life memories which occupy and intrude upon the realm of the material, factual world hammers home the point that the memories of the slaves and our connection to them are alive and inseparable from our existence. Such treatment in the narration of this story must be regarded as Morrison's response to the repression of memory in slave narratives, in which fiction is separate from fact.

So real, in fact are Sethe's memories, that the community reacts to them. Drivers whip their horses into a gallop when they pass Sethe. Sethe's alienation from the community, then, is the direct result of her inability to relate the story. Her vain attempt to search for an audience within the community is shown when she purchases a tombstone for her daughter and has the word "Beloved" engraved upon it. The tombstone is dearly bought—she has no money so she sells her own body to obtain the engraving: "She thought it would be enough . . . to answer one more preacher, one more abolitionist and a town full of disgust" (5). Like Brent, Sethe is desperately consumed with the desire to tell the story—not simply to herself, but to others. Brent and Sethe must explain why they did what they did. Brent explains why she ran away, why slavery was so horrible that she hid in a small hole in the wall for seven years in order to escape her master's bed. Sethe must explain to an entire town disgusted by her actions. The word "Beloved" on the tombstone is her unheard defense: she loved her child even though she killed it. Still, even this expensively bought word is not enough to quell the disgust. This judgment coming from the Black community is the result of their binary thinking: Sethe is different from them and her difference makes her inferior and degraded. Where such thinking exists, the story cannot and will not be released and censorship is the result.

How does the narration work under the conditions of Sethe's censorship? As readers can see in the passage above, the narrator has remembered Sethe's response to the ghost and reports it. In so doing, the narrator gives readers the background necessary to understand Sethe's actions, which she does not explain herself. Here the benefits of the narrator as omniscient narrator, as opposed to the first person narrator, so often used in slave narratives is evident. M.H. Abrams notes that in the first person narrative, the narrator "I" is "only a fortuitous witness and auditor of the matters he relates"; the narration is limited to what the narrator "knows, experiences, infers, or can find out by talking to other characters" (167). The slave narrator can only report what he witnesses: he cannot report to his or her audience the inner feelings of the other slaves without violating the expected limits of the first person narrator (and he does this only at the risk of representing a fiction). As a result, the narrator must diminish the "I"—the thoughts, feelings of the other slaves represented in his narrative. Furthermore, the narrator must diminish his own "I" in the attempt to represent the slave body as a whole.[14] He or she may do this, as Douglass does in the first part of his narrative, by recounting short anecdotes about other slaves which divert the reader from his own story. Although the anecdotes prove that the abuses of slavery Douglass experienced were common to all slaves, these anecdotes do not do full justice to the lives of those represented in these tales.

On the other hand, the omniscient narrator knows everything that "needs to be known," all of the thoughts, emotions, and motives are available to him and he is free to move "in time and place, to shift from character to character, and to report their speech, doings, and the states of consciousness" (Abrams, 166). As a result, the omniscient narrator has the power to represent the "I's of various characters: their points of view need not be diminished. Morrison certainly takes full advantage of the powers of the omniscient narrator when she unfolds the tale of Denver's birth. Whereas in the first passage quoted above the narrator functions as a historian, reporting the background material needed to understand Sethe's behavior, in the passage on Denver's birth, the narrator begins to move between time and space, from the mind of mother to daughter through a body of language.

This fascinating chapter on Denver's birth begins by revealing untold secrets. In so doing, it focuses on the interior, private self of Denver—a side that could not be told in the slave narratives. Denver steals away to this place where her "imagination produce[s] its own hunger and its own food" (28). The forest boxwood where she hides becomes a symbol of her interior world and also the literal place where her interior can exist. Stepping out of this enclosed place, one day, Denver steps into a "told story," her mother's memory of her birth (29). As Denver walks back to her house from the woods, she remembers her mother's walk through the forest carrying her in her belly.

The narrator shifts from Denver's point of view to Sethe's with little warn-ing. We are told that Denver judges the distance from her forest to the house in order to carefully synchronize the relation of the story with the space she walks. The merger between the time and space of Denver walking in the woods, Sethe telling the story to Denver, and Sethe walking in the woods all merge in this sentence:

> And to get to the part of the part of the story she liked best, she had to start way back [in the forest]: hear the birds in the thick woods, the crunch of leaves underfoot; see her mother making her way up into the hills . . . How Sethe was walking on two feet meant for standing still . . . But she could not, would not, stop, for when she did the little antelope rammed her with horns and pawed the ground of her womb with impa-tient hooves. . . . (30–31)

This passage begins with the personal pronoun "she," which refers at first to Denver and then to her mother. Denver imagines, as she walks home, the time and space of her mother: and she hears the birds and the crunch of leaves in her own environment, even as she imagines it to be her mother's. The narra-tive then pauses to give a sentence that reflects the telling of the story, her mother's relation of the story to her. The sentence replicates a summary of the memory "how Sethe was walking on two feet meant for standing still." This statement is an evaluation which Denver or her mother could have made upon its relation, at a separate time. The sentence marks the transition between consciousnesses and also serves to notify readers that Denver is reminding herself of the story so that she can inhabit the memory. In the final sentence of this passage, the "she" becomes Sethe and Denver becomes the antelope, ramming her mother's womb. Denver's metonymical walk begins in a room in the forest which resembles the womb, and then the walk continues in the womb of Denver's memory and the literal womb in her mother's belly.

The maternal imagery of mother and child continues as the narrator jumps to Sethe's experience carrying Denver and thinking about her own mother. Sethe remembers having her own mother pointed out to her by another child. Her mother is indistinguishable from the bodies of many slaves similarly stooped to pick cotton in the fields: "What she [Sethe] saw was a cloth hat as opposed to a straw one, singularity enough in that world of cooing women each of whom was called Ma'am" (30). As Denver kicks in her mother's womb, Sethe remembers her relationship to the body of slaves who all became mother. The narrator moves on to the next memory Sethe has, a memory which connects the boxwood, the antelope, and the women in the fields. Sethe remembers the body of slaves dancing and singing. Sometimes "they danced the ante-lope . . . They shifted shapes and became something other. Some unchained, demanding other whose feet knew her pulse better than she did. Just like this one in her stomach" (31). The antelope in her belly knows (remembers) the ante-lope the slaves dance. Denver knows this pulse simply because each of the bodies remember, and can never be divorced from, their freedom and the cultural patterns which determine and distinguish the shapes of their lives. Cultural memory and individual memory is here passed down from mother to child and perhaps greater than this is a life force itself that is passed down from generation to generation. Chained or unchained, it always dances and it is always free and it always remembers. The function of the omniscient narrator is to make such connections visible, connections of which the characters are only semi-conscious. The passage which follows reveals the limits of the characters' access to what is unspoken: the omniscient narrator fills in the gaps for readers. Sethe's walk in the forest, and her run away from her master, is interrupted by the discovery of another:

> The voice, saying, "Who's in there?" was all she [Sethe] needed to know that she was about to be discovered by a white-boy. That he too had mossy teeth, an appetite. That on a ridge of pine near the Ohio River, trying to get to her three children, one of whom was starving for the food she carried . . . she was not to have an easeful death. . . . Suddenly she was eager for his eyes, to bite into them; to gnaw his cheek. "I was hungry," she told Denver. (31)

Here the narrator continues to juxtapose three different times and spaces. The focus of the narrative is on Sethe's time and space. However, the narrative juxtaposes this time and place with the event of Sethe's relation of this memory to her daughter. The third time and space, which is diminished in this passage, is the time when Denver is walking through the forest remembering what her mother told her. What is interesting in this passage is how the omniscient narrator reveals the difference between what Sethe remembers and what she tells to Denver. When Sethe hears the voice of a stranger, she immediately suspects that her interlocutor is a White boy. The omniscient narrator begins to reveal Sethe's memories which cause fear and suspicion. The words "that he too had mossy teeth, an appetite" refer to the memory Sethe has of the White boys who raped her, whom she describes as having "mossy teeth" (70). These boys are her slave masters from whom she runs away. She escaped after they raped her and drank her milk. When Sethe encounters the stranger in the woods, she thinks about the strange appetite of the rapists she left behind. She also thinks about the appetite of her children, who need what is left of her body to nurture them.

Appetite, then, is on her mind while she starves for food. She has an appetite for leaving the slave holders, for feeding her children, and for living a free life. She turns her hunger for life into an appetite to do harm, to eat the other, dangerous stranger instead of being eaten herself: "she was eager for his eyes, to bite them." The omniscient narrator reveals Sethe's thoughts and memories, and then tells the readers that the only thing she told her daughter is simply "I was hungry." Sethe does not tell Denver about her fear of being raped or killed, nor does she tell her that these memories of her rape haunted her even at the event of Denver's birth. Instead, she only remembers and relates to Denver her appetite for food and for life. Ostensibly, this is why Denver likes to remember the occasion of her birth; Sethe's omission is what imbues the memory with enough light to be a source of joy to Denver. This is the crucial difference between what Denver remembers as she walks through the forest and what happened to Sethe when she walked in the forest; it is the difference between speaking for the other and for the self. In speaking for Sethe and Denver, the omniscient narrator follows the patterns of the memories as they occur in their minds rather than to unfold the story as a logical progression of chronological time (as a slave narrative grounded in relating the facts with precision and objectivity seeks to do). In this sense, the narrator finds a written language for the images in Denver and Sethe's memories. The language of this passage is typical of the language in *Beloved* in the sense that it is preoccupied primarily with what characters remember as opposed to what they say; and it is concerned with relating the memories as they sometimes occur. The transition of memory as it moves through time and space, the loss of its parts to censorship, and the disorganization of its narrative is the focus of this novel and the pattern of its narrative structure.

In the passage above, readers may identify the way that material reality is always placed in the prism of memory; it never exists as a concrete, objective place in and of itself. There is no stationary "place" in this passage: the forests of Sethe and Denver are displaced in this narrative so that they can only be seen through the mind. Where does this scene occur? There is no tangible place, since the narrative moves through memory and imagination. The fact that the narration moves only through the mind must also be regarded as a challenge to the idea that any slave narrative can separate reality from memory and imagination. When the omniscient narrator takes on the very pattern and thought of the unspoken memories of Sethe and Denver, it writes not for itself, but for them; in listening and relating the memories it becomes the perfect receptor for their authentic, unspoken voices.

Although Sethe does not have the kind of audience in Denver that she has in the narrator at this stage in the novel, she continues to search for it. As she continues her quest, she receives more memories about the past, memories which hurt, and for which no audience in sight can heal. Sethe learns from her lover, Paul D, that her husband had gone crazy.

With the weight of this memory, she staggers to the Clearing, a place where healing had taken place in the past. Sethe's journey to the Clearing prefigures her own restoration and release of her memory to an audience. The Clearing, now vacant, had been the place where the Black community met and healed one another, under the direction of the minister, Baby Suggs. Sethe now sits in the Clearing where she remembers Baby Suggs' sermon. Her sermon triggers the kind of healing which an audience has the power to give: the merging and emerging formation of a single body united in language. The omniscient narrator again tells the story of this sermon. Baby Suggs invites the children to laugh. Then she tells the men to dance. Then she tells the women to cry. Soon the roles are mixed as each part of this whole acquires the role of the other. "Women stopped crying and danced; men sat down and cried; children danced. . . ." (88). Baby Suggs speaks:

> "Here," she said, "in this here place, we flesh; flesh that weeps laughs; flesh that dances on bare feet in grass. Love it. Yonder they do not love your flesh. They despise it. They don't love your eyes; they'd just as soon pick em out. No more do they love the skin on your back. Yonder they flay it. . . . More than your life-holding womb and your life-giving private parts, hear me now, and love your heart. For this is the prize." Saying no more, she stood up then and danced with her twisted hip the rest of what her heart had to say. . . . (88–89).

As Sethe sits in the Clearing remembering the sermons of long ago, she longed for them (89). Surely her longing was for the way in which the slaves came together as one body, crying and dancing and laughing for one another: the parts of the assembly assume responsibility for and empathizing fully with the other parts. The tears of the mothers become the tears of the children and the joy of the children becomes the joy of the men and the women. The voice of this body is Baby Suggs: and as the voice of the people she tells their story. They have been persecuted. They have not been loved by others. She voices a litany of complaints and unspoken thoughts of this assembly of slaves; thoughts which cannot be communicated to those who persecute them, thoughts and memories for which there is no audience. These thoughts are articulated and released. Loving one another, as Baby Suggs suggests, means identifying with the other as one's self. Baby Suggs ends the sermon by speaking with her own body, articulating the joy they must feel after finding release. She represents the heart of this body because she gives the body of slaves her heart and articulates a heart for them.

It is therefore significant that Baby Suggs is dead when Sethe begins her quest for an audience: there is no heart in the community any more because it has forgotten how to come together and how to listen and love so that these memories from the past can be released through a spokesperson and a body (of people) that speaks. Equally significant, is the fact that Baby Suggs stops preaching after Sethe murders her child. The omniscient narrator reports: "Her [Baby Suggs] faith, her love, her imagination and her great big old heart began to collapse twenty-eight days after her daughter in-law [Sethe] arrived" (89). Baby Suggs gives up after witnessing the murder, surely, a scene (as the slave narratives put it) too terrible to relate. Baby Suggs can no longer speak and she can no longer love. But more to the point, the community can no longer speak and they no longer love one another; they become fragmented.

When Paul D. shows up and becomes Sethe's lover, Sethe has another chance to find an audience. But Stamp Paid, a member of the community, reveals Sethe's secret to him (154–155). In astonished disbelief, Paul D. confronts Sethe, expecting her to deny that she murdered her child. For the first time, she seeks to put into words the horrible images in her mind. What emerges from her lips is her incoherent, twisted story. Her narration is noticeably bent by the weight of conforming to the expectations of her audience, Paul D., whose expectation is that this story would not be told. The omniscient narrator comments on Sethe's verbal narration of her own story: "Circling, circling, now she was gnawing something else instead of getting to the point" (162). Finally, the narrator intervenes, telling readers what Sethe could not say to Paul D concerning her explanation: "Sethe knew that the circle she was making around the room, him, the subject would remain one" (162). The narrator goes on to explain what Sethe cannot: that when the slaveholders came to take her and her children back into slavery, she heard "hummingbirds" and decided that she would put her children where "no one could hurt them" (162).

Sethe finally discovers the means by which she could relate her story, and the audience to whom she could relate it after Paul D. leaves her. Beloved, the woman who mysteriously appears from nowhere, has the appetite for Sethe's stories. Furthermore, Sethe soon discovers that Beloved knows what Sethe does not tell her. When Beloved hums a song that Sethe made up and sang to her children years before Beloved arrived, Sethe makes this discovery (176). Furthermore, Sethe decides that Beloved is the same child she murdered; she is her daughter come back to life. Because Sethe realizes that Beloved knows her thoughts, Sethe decides that she does not have to explain verbally what happened; Beloved will already know what happened through the nonverbal transference of memories: "Be nice to think first, before I talk to her, let her know I know. Think about all I ain't got to remember no more" (182). The answer to the call Sethe and Denver had given to the murdered baby girl was being answered. And because Beloved and Sethe can communicate through memory, Sethe no longer has to explain verbally what happened or to construct a narrative of memory acceptable to an audience.

Mae Henderson correctly links Sethe's project of finding a way of remembering and telling the past to Morrison's project of remembering and relating the past:

> Lacking a discourse of her own, Sethe's task is to transform the residual images ("rememories") of her past into a historical discourse shaped by narrativity. These images, however, remain for a time disembodied—without form, sequence, or meaning . . . Like Morrison, Sethe must learn to represent the unspeakable and unspoken in language—and more precisely, as narrative. (67)

In other words, when Sethe finds that Beloved remembers her story, she discovers what Morrison calls in her essay "literary archeology." And, as Henderson implies, Sethe becomes the figure which represents Morrison's own search for the language to convey the slave's narrative. At the same time, Sethe is the product of Morrison's search: it is through literary archeology that Morrison reconstructs Margaret Garner/ Sethe's life. In this way, a seamless transmission of history: the representation of what happened in the past passes on from Margaret Garner to Morrison and from Morrison to Sethe; and from Sethe to Beloved. As each member of this chain finds an audience that receives and relates the truth about the past, boundaries between past and present, fiction and fact, author and subject are blurred.

It is at this juncture in the novel that distinctions between one character and another are blurred through the transition of memory. As Henderson notes, the unspoken which passes between Sethe and Beloved reveals that they are one and the same person. Beloved is the embodiment of Sethe's past which she must confront (74–75). At the same time, Beloved is not simply a metaphor, but she is a literal character who occupies a physical body. The character of Beloved, then, becomes the perfect audience for Sethe. Their unspoken discourse symbolically represents Sethe's living in the past. It also represents her location of an audience outside of herself. In her "daughter" Beloved, Sethe finds someone who knows her song without being taught it; the other (Beloved) thus becomes one with Sethe through this unspoken discourse and receives the authentic and complete story of what Sethe experienced (her I) and saw (through her eyes).[15] And we realize that all along Beloved has spoken for Sethe. The questions she asks about Sethe's history ("Where your diamonds?" "Your woman she never fix up your hair?" 63) reveal and verbalize the need for the past, Sethe's past, to be spoken.

Denver too becomes part of this trinity, as she also participates in the discourse of the unspoken with her sister and her mother. I would like to extend Henderson's observation that Denver represents Sethe's future (75). Denver and Beloved are not only the past and the future but they represent Sethe's memory and relation of that memory respectively. As I mentioned earlier, Beloved begins with Sethe's desperate attempts to release and relate her memory. Her attempts remain incomplete until she realizes she does not have to communicate verbally. In another realm, then, she allows herself to be fully conscious of the means by which her memories have already been passed on. Her daughter, Beloved makes her aware of this other realm. If Beloved helps Sethe to remember, then it is her daughter Denver, who helps Sethe to relay the message. It is Denver who finally leaves the house and gets help from the community; she tells Sethe's story and the community rallies around Sethe to heal her. As one body (a body that had not been united since Baby Suggs retired) the women of the community pray for Sethe, dispersing the memories that haunted her. If Denver and Beloved represent Sethe, then what Sethe does (in the figure of Denver reaching out to the community)[16] is to force the community to come to terms with memories (about slavery that disgusted them) that had prevented them from healing and loving one another unconditionally as a body. As long as one member of this body (Sethe) was excluded or one member's memories were too awful to relate, the healing could not be complete. By finding a way of remembering and relating these memories, Sethe becomes the communal healer and the catalyst for the revival of healing which took place on the Clearing.[17] Indeed, after Denver reaches out to the community, the women of the community come together to pray for Sethe. Together, they raise the specter of the Clearing as they exorcise the demon of Sethe's memory. As one voice, they sing:

> For Sethe it was as though the Clearing has come to her with all its heat and simmering leaves, where the voices of women searched for the right combination, the key, the code, the sound that broke the back of words. Building voice upon voice until they

found it, and when they did it was a wave of sound wide enough to sound deep water and knock the pods off chestnut trees. (261)

At last, Sethe is included in the body of voices; at last, she is the recipient of their healing; at last, the community has gathered the strength to face the worst memories produced by slavery. In the end, the result is that Beloved takes her leave of Sethe (258–259).

Like Sethe, Morrison too becomes a community healer as she taps into the realm of the imagination and memory to bring the authentic story of the past to the present. In telling the story of the beloved slaves who died, she addresses the unwillingness of the Black community to confront images unspeakable and unspoken. By remembering and telling, Morrison provides a model for healing among her readers even as she becomes the catalyst for it.

The preparation for Morrison's role as a healer began when she wrote *The Bluest Eye*. Even then, Morrison was developing a method of gaining access to that which is unspeakable and unspoken, and then finding a means to represent those images in writing. In the last section of this chapter, I will examine closely the fullest development and release of this language in *Beloved* and trace its development from *The Bluest Eye*.

Shortly after Sethe realizes that Beloved knows, without telling her, what she remembers, she begins in earnest to communicate with both daughters in the unspoken. The four chapters which follow this discovery are what Henderson calls "the poetry chapters," where this language is found. Each member of this trinity releases her memories in a kind of unspoken monologue. In the third chapter their memories are joined. A full analysis of each monologue is beyond the scope of this chapter. However, the form, and not the content, reveals the nature of the written language Morrison uses to convey the unspoken. And a sample of the monologues demonstrates that the form she uses is consistent. I cite a passage from the final chapter in which the monologues of the three women are combined:

Your face is mine. /Do you forgive me? Will you stay? You safe here now./Where are the men without skin?/ Out there. Way off./ Can they get in here?/No. They tried that once, but I stopped them. They won't ever come back./One of them was in the house I was in. He hurt me./They can't hurt us no more. (215)

Because the pronouns do not have referents, it is difficult to tell who is speaking and to what the conversation refers. The statement, "Your face is mine," may be spoken by any of the three women. Since they are all related, they each have the faces of the other; they each belong to the other. In the next line, it may very well be that Sethe asks her daughter Beloved to forgive her for murdering her, assures her of her safety, and asks her to stay. But if Sethe does utter this line, then does she utter the first line as well? Or, is there a dialogue which occurs between the first line and the second line, with Beloved declaring the Sethe is hers and Sethe asking for forgiveness? The boundaries between the languages are unclear: it is uncertain who owns the words. At the same time, the women speak in different contexts. For example, when Sethe (?) utters "Do you forgive me?" she is clearly speaking about her daughter and to her daughter. But is her daughter Beloved? Scholars such as Jean Wyatt and Robert Broad have demonstrated that Beloved is also the ghost of a slave girl who died on a slave ship. This ghost mistakes her mother for Sethe. Perhaps Beloved is speaking to her own mother who abandoned her. Perhaps Beloved thinks Sethe is her mother asking her for forgiveness. The "men without skins" are the white men who enslaved Beloved on the slave ship and they are the men who enslaved Sethe.

On another level, the women may not be making reference to the slave ship but to the special discourse in which they communicate. Their collective concern with the men without skins obtaining access to their space "They tried that once, but I stopped them" is a reference to the realm in which only they can speak and understand one another: the unspeakable unspoken. What is remarkable about this dialogue is that the words speak both for the self and the other.[18] In other words, even when the women speak in different contexts (even as they speak in the same context), the women understand each other. As a linguistic body, the words demarcate the experiences of each of the slaves at the same time that they speak for the whole.[19] Space and time collapse and remain distinct.

What Morrison has done is to present the realm of memory in written form. This written form includes the recession of the omniscient narrator. The narrator no longer serves the function of contextualizing, editing, or connecting which it does earlier in the novel. The recession of the narrator marks Sethe's success in immersing herself in the realm where she merges with her audience at the same time that it marks a representation in language of what Sethe experiences. Previously the omniscient narrator had served as the intercessor between this realm and the page, placing in writing an ordered, edited form of what was unspoken, making connections for the reader that Sethe herself could not make with other characters. When the omniscient narrator recedes, readers are given fuller access to what Sethe experiences and what she reveals and what she remembers. The implication of this linguistic gesture of the self (Sethe) speaking to the self (who is the other) without being censored or edited or contextualized is an important one. It symbolizes the arrival and transmission of the authentic words of the slaves on paper, unedited and unconformed to the expectations of their audiences.

Compare the language of the character Beloved with that of Pecola's madness in The Bluest Eye. In both cases, the unspoken is represented. Pecola's language is represented as a dialogue that occurs in her mind. As a character who is silent most of her life, her mad talk, unspoken, is the only access readers have to the inner recesses of her mind. There are two differences between the language used for Pecola and Beloved. First, the omniscient narrator intervenes more forcefully; at the end of the dialogue, the narrator informs readers, albeit briefly, about the nature of her dialogue. There is no such intervention in the poetic chapters of Beloved. Secondly, the position of Pecola's dialogue is lower than that of Beloved's. Pecola's dialogue is posited as the unfortunate result of her lack of verbal communication with the community; her dialogue is insular—no one in her community has access to it. In Beloved, the dialogue between Beloved and Sethe is the goal of the text; it represents a kind of freedom for Sethe who is finally able to tell her story and to find an audience; and it represents a discursive site where a community of slaves and their memories reside. Pecola is a version of Beloved, but twenty years later, her mad talk is no longer madness and she speaks for all (and not just herself); in this sense, she speaks with a greater degree of power.[20]

Beloved/Pecola's growth bears a metonymical relationship to the growth of Morrison's own voice as a writer. The Bluest Eye (1970) was her first publication. And she wrote it at a time when her marriage had ended around 1964. It was a time when, as she says: "It was as though I had nothing left but my imagination. I had no will, no judgment, no perspective, no power, no authority, no self— but this brutal sense of irony, melancholy, and a trembling respect for words" (175).[21] However, between the time of the publication of her first novel, and that of Beloved, she had published three additional novels and had won accolades and attention for her work. Indeed, Beloved earned the 1988 Pulitzer Prize for Fiction, one of the highest honors bestowed upon her by the critical and academic communities.

More to the point, however, the growth of Beloved/Pecola's voice also parallels the collective growth of Black women's voices and audiences within those two decades. At the time of the publication of The Bluest Eye, Black women's literature was scarcely the subject of critical and academic attention. But a community of Black women writers, Paule Marshall, Ntozake Shange,

Alice Walker, and Morrison among them, emerged during that period of time, captured the attention of increasingly wider audiences with their own work, and reminded audiences of the work of their predecessors. As Cheryl Wall notes:

> Over the last two decades, Afro-American women have written themselves into the national consciousness. Their work is widely read, frequently taught, and increasingly the object of critical inquiry. Wherever it is met, black women's writing elicits impassioned responses from readers across boundaries of race and gender. (1)

Surely the growing tolerance (and the growing optimism about this tolerance) of the academic discursive community to listen to this literature is one leap into the future.

· 4 ·

"AND THE VOICE OF HIS WORDS LIKE THE VOICE OF A MULTITUDE"[1]: SPEAKING AND WRITING FOR THE OTHER REVISITED

In Chapter 3, I discuss one of the central motifs in Toni Morrison's *Beloved*: how the self speaks for the other. This occurs when the omniscient narrator gives voice to the unspoken thoughts of the characters and when the main characters, Sethe, Beloved, and Denver, each become the vehicles through which the unspoken thoughts of others find release. Sethe finds that Beloved and Denver possess the ability and the strength to remember and relate her memories of slavery. Beloved, readers come to discover, is the living embodiment of slavery's untold past; every word she utters (or does not utter) speaks for and about those memories in general, and about Sethe's memories in particular. Denver relates Sethe's painful story to the community: an act which Sethe cannot bring herself to do. In short, Chapter 3 reveals how the voice—the essence of a human presence (and past) as opposed to the language used to represent it—is communicated for one character by another.

In this chapter, I focus on the linguistic material of Beloved's speaking voice, as opposed to the presence it represents. Specifically, I examine how her voice represents a chorus of the multitude of slaves who use a variety of tongues. In so doing, I describe the grammatical features of the language used to represent the voice of Beloved. Such a focus involves an analysis of the **looks** of her language, the discovery and description of its linguistic features, and how these features may be placed on a continuum ranging from Standard to Nonstandard written and spoken English. Indeed, Beloved utters two different varieties of English. Her spoken language can be accommodated to competing and conflicting linguistic theories of the history of Early Black English. Secondly, Beloved's language in the "poetic" section can be compared to the unedited writing of slaves, who are unfamiliar with the conventions of written English which enable them to write clearly for audiences. Beloved's peculiar words represent that which is unrecorded: the histories of the slaves in their own spoken and written words; these are the **acts** investigated in this chapter.

The first section of this chapter examines the language Beloved uses outside of the poetic chapters. The last section of this paper examines Beloved's language inside the poetic chapters.

I begin my analysis with Beloved's talk, and why, as Paul D observes, it is "funny" and even aberrant (234). The syntax, lexicon, and grammar of Beloved's question: "Your woman she never fix your hair?" are some of the features which make her language peculiar (60). Her lexicon, in this sentence and elsewhere reveals her linguistic strategy to force a few words to serve as signifiers for a variety of meaning. Beloved leaves out the term "mother," choosing to use instead "your woman." Another example is her choice of the verb "fix," to signify the verb "comb." "Fix" is used in similar ways in other passages of this novel. For instance, Beloved uses "fix" to mean "tie" when she says: "The shoe strings don't fix!" (65). Elsewhere she uses "fix" to indicate "caress" and "heal": "Didn't I fix her neck? . . . I kissed her neck, I didn't choke it . . . (101). In another instance, she uses the term "diamonds" to indicate the words "earrings" and "crystal" ("Where your diamonds?") (58). And Beloved avoids using the verb "cry" when she asks Sethe, "You finished with your eyes" (175). Finally,

Sethe refrains from referring to the specific action she requests when she asks Paul D to "touch her on her inside part . . ." (116).

In addition to this strained lexicon, the existence of the pronominal apposition is another nonstandard feature of Beloved's language. According to linguists Ralph Fasold and Walt Wolfram, "pronominal apposition is the construction in which a pronoun is used in apposition to the noun subject of the sentence" (81). In Beloved's question, the pronoun "she" repeats the subject, "your woman."

The absence of tense markers is another salient feature of her language. The context in which Beloved says "Your woman she never fix your hair?" reveals the need for the past tense of the verb "fix." Beloved's question concerns a person who is absent from her presence, and therefore from the present. In the same way, Beloved's observation that the "shoe strings don't fix" refers to a journey she made in the past.

It is important to note Sethe's reaction to Beloved's question, since it reveals the linguistic differences between the two speakers. First, Sethe responds with a question that seeks clarification: "My woman? You mean my mother?" (60). (This question is one of several asked of Beloved for clarification.[2] Sethe's question indicates that the term "woman" is not a common signifier for "mother" in their community.

In addition to the substitution of the word "mother" for "your woman," Sethe's response, "She never fixed my hair nor nothing" includes other changes in the syntax and lexicon (60). Sethe's statement is notable for the extent to which it fails to reproduce Beloved's sentence structure. For example, Sethe's sentence uses the suffix -ed to mark the past tense of the verb "fix." Also absent is the pronominal apposition found in Beloved's question. And unlike Beloved, Sethe does not use the verb "fix" often; more to the point, her vocabulary is larger than Beloved's. The multiple negative which Sethe adds in her sentence ("never, "nor," "nothing") is frequently used by other characters such as Baby Suggs (244), Ella (186), and even Schoolteacher (227); it renders Sethe's language more common rather than more peculiar.

What Sethe does is to substitute Beloved's grammatical, lexical, and syntactical features for those which are more common to her own speech patterns, and those in her surrounding community. Beloved and Sethe's language may be placed on a continuum between less common and more common nonstandard forms of English.

Is Beloved's unusual diction a general feature of her language? Perhaps the most puzzling feature of Beloved's language is her inconsistent use of the nonstandard language discussed above. For example, she does use tense mark-ers according to the standard rules of English when she uses the past forms of the verbs "do" and "fix" to describe her response to Sethe's choking (101). Another example of Beloved's use of standard forms of English occurs when she says "What is velvet?" (77). However, since Beloved rarely talks, her string of nonstandard sentences constitute significant portions of her language. In general, Beloved's inconsistent use of past tense markers (see pg. 75 for more examples), her strange choices of lexicon, and her use of unusual nonstandard forms characterize her language.

The differences between Beloved's language and Sethe's may be further described as the differences between two idiolects. J.L. Dillard defines an idio-lect as the "characteristic speech pattern of an individual" (301). I would also suggest that the features of Beloved's language are so idiosyncratic (while Sethe's language is so common to her community) that the differences between the language used by these two characters are also meant to suggest the differ-ences between two varieties of language. Dillard defines "variety" as "a relatively neutral designation for something between a language and an idiolect" (304). Beloved speaks one variety while Sethe and the community speak another.

The margins of difference between Beloved's language and the language of the community and between idiolect and language are indeterminate; yet, it is this margin of difference which is signified by Beloved's language. In other words, there is enough peculiarity in Beloved's language to suggest a linguistic distinction from her community which falls within the unknown margin of difference between an idiolect and a language.

It is no coincidence that the subject of this margin of difference is implic-itly raised with Beloved's question ("Your woman she . . .") which epitomizes her linguistic difference. This question is used rhetorically in the novel to raise the issue of linguistic difference in Sethe's past. When she asks Sethe about her mother, Beloved triggers Sethe's memories about her mother's tongue, the tongue she spoke when she was younger. In the process, the subject of the varieties of language spoken by the Black community is raised.

The memory occurs when Sethe thinks about her mother's death and the support she received from Nan, the woman who knew Sethe's mother:

> [Nan] used different words. Words Sethe understood then   but   could neither recall nor repeat now . . . What Nan told her she had forgotten, along with the language she told   it in. The same language her ma'am spoke, and which   would never come back. (62)

This passage does not reveal the name of this language. Nor do we know how long Sethe remembered it or how many other slaves spoke it. However, what is clear is that more than one variety of language existed within this slave community. Sethe speaks two of these varieties; one is her first unknown tongue, and the other is her current tongue.

This passage reflects the transition from the unknown African tongues spoken by the slaves before they were captured to the variety of English spoken by the Black Community at the moment of Sethe's reflection, years after slavery was over. Nan and Sethe's mother were slaves who experienced the Middle Passage; they could have spoken an African language. However, they also could have spoken an admixture (more or less) of African and English languages, a variety of English (or an African tongue) which Sethe no longer remembers.

Since Beloved also represents the experiences of the slaves during the Middle Passage, as Robert Broad, Jean Wyatt, and Jennifer Holden-Kirwan suggest—as well as Sethe's past, as Mae Henderson suggests (see Chapter 3)—Beloved's language represents figuratively the variety of languages spoken by the Africans during their passage from slavery to freedom. More specifically, her language dramatizes the transition from one language to another which Sethe herself made. Beloved's language also represents literally these unknown varieties of Early Black English spoken by Sethe and the slaves.

At first glance, this last statement is a paradox. How can this be? While it is true that there are competing theories about the origin of Black English, the features of Beloved's language can be accommodated to these theories. My discussion of this accommodation begins with a review of these competing histories and incorporates a second examination of her grammar. In the process of this discussion, I hope to answer the following questions: Why is Beloved's language marked by these particular features of nonstandard language? Why is it inconsistent, containing standard as well as nonstandard features? Why does her language simulate baby talk? Why is she the only one who speaks this language among all of the characters?

Linguists classify theories concerning the origin of Black English according to their basic tenets. Two of the main schools of thought are the substrate hypothesis and the superstrate hypothesis.[3] The substrate hypothesis claims that the native languages of those Africans had a strong impact on the language they spoke when they arrived and stayed in America. The superstrate hypothesis contends that the contribution of the African languages was minimal and that nonstandard English spoken by the Europeans had a greater impact on the formation of Black English.

One of the best known theories of the substrate hypothesis which gained currency three decades ago is found in J.L. Dillard's *Black English*. Dillard argues that "differences from other English dialects are traceable to . . . language-contact phenomena associated with the West African slave trade and with European maritime expansion in general, and to survivals from West African languages" (ix).[4] Slaves learned a lingua franca, probably a pidgin (a basic mixture of two languages acquired as a second language for both groups) Portuguese language from the slave traders while still in Africa. When they arrived in America, the slaves added English, and new generations of slaves began to speak this form of "Plantation Creole" (a pidgin is called a creole when it becomes the first language of the new generation). Over time, varieties of this creole were spoken by both Black and White Americans.[5] Dillard also argues that these varieties of English are related to Gullah, the dialect of the Sea Islands.[6]

Superstratists, on the other hand, counter that most of the slaves fully learned the dialect of their new environment (Schneider 24–25). The differences attributed to Black English come from the nonstandard dialects of English learned from surrounding Whites, many of whom were illiterate (Schneider, 24–25). Thus, the language spoken by Black Americans depends more upon regional differences which are influenced by social and economical factors rather than to the traces left by Creole. Furthermore, many of the nonstandard features are attributed to older forms of British dialect (Burling, 112). The clash of these two theories has produced two important results. First, linguists have adopted a wide spectrum of opinions between the two extreme viewpoints. Some of the leading linguists have sought an intermediary position.[7] Secondly, proponents from both sides challenge each other to produce definitive data to support their arguments. For example, superstratist Edgar Schneider rebuts Dillard's assertion that all slaves learned one pidgin on the slave ships, or on the plantations; Schneider argues that the circumstances would have dictated a continuum of linguistic outcomes dependent upon the population of Blacks and the conditions on the slave ships and plantations. He raises the following questions about how the acquisition of a Creole would have occurred under the conditions described by Dillard:

A new and different phrasing of the central question is needed: not if but to what extent did creolization occur among American slaves? Were such processes locally restricted, and if so, where can we expect them to have been more marked or, alternatively, not influential? Was the resulting speech form stable enough to be called a creole? . . . Which linguistic variables were affected, and in what way? (41)

Many or few of the slaves may have learned a creole; and this form of creole may have influenced other varieties of English, or it may not have influenced them at all; and this "creole" may have been only partially influenced by the first languages of the slaves.

How can the process of second language acquisition for the slaves who crossed the Middle Passage be represented when a consensus about such basic details is lacking? The complexity of Beloved's characterization somehow accommodates both the substrate and superstrate theories. At the same time, the indeterminacy of her characterization accommodates the concerns raised by Schneider about the multiplicity of scenarios which could have occurred in the development of Black English.

Beloved represents a multitude of slaves who crossed the Middle Passage; yet, at the same time, she represents a single individual who moves and exists in postbellum North America.[8] She does not exist in a fixed linear time and space. This is why the language that she uses can loosely accommodate a multiplicity of scenarios. She represents the condition of a multitude of slaves who learned the new language(s) at various stages during the Middle Passage: on the shores of Africa, in the ships at sea, or on the shores of America. At the same time she represents the single individual who speaks or learns one language. The inconsistency of Beloved's language, and particularly her ability to use, on occasion, language that conforms to the rules of standard English could signify a transition that she is making from a pidgin language to another variety of English. Furthermore, the fact that only Beloved uses her peculiar brand of English, rather than the other slaves in her community, conforms to the degree of uncertainty scholars have about the impact of such language on the larger speech community of American (and especially Black American) English. Such a depiction echoes the widely held belief that the early history of Black English and Creole had little impact upon the current composition of Black English.[9]

There are more specific features of Beloved's nonstandard language which raise the specter of the creole theory. A second analysis of Beloved's sentence, "Your woman she never fix your hair?" and of Beloved's language in general supports this conclusion.

The research produced by Geneva Smitherman, William Labov, and Derek Bickerman supports the idea that certain features of Beloved's language are aberrant. For very different reasons, each theory conforms to the suggestion that these features are a form of Early Black English: although, as I discuss, the notion of what "early" is changes with each theoretical context.

Smitherman contends that the pronominal apposition, the absence of tense markers, and the absence of the auxillary "do" in questions—all of which occur in Beloved's question, are linguistic features which were grafted onto an early form of Black English from the rules of West African languages. She reasons that West African languages such as Ibo, Yoruba, and Hausa all have these syntactical commonalities, although they differ in vocabulary. Therefore, a multitude of slaves who spoke different languages could have imposed the structural rules of their languages upon the English language, thereby receiving the same results: a form of Black English in existence today (6–7). William Labov argues that the absence of past tense markers from Black English is odd and "early" for different reasons than Smitherman. In Labov's analysis, the absence of the tense markers in Beloved's language can be indicative of the form of Black English used most often in the early stages of a Black child's linguistic development. He finds, as does Burling (52) and Fasold (60), that the past tense marker -ed is part of the Black dialect, although it is often not pronounced by its speakers. However, Labov found that some children cannot recognize -ed as a past tense marker and use it effectively in reading (32). Surely the absence of the -ed in a significant portion of Beloved's language is reflective of the fact that Beloved is illiterate and the ghost of a child.

In addition to the theories detailed above, a third theory, proposed by Derek Bickerton, also lends support to the idea that some of Beloved's features are an early form of Black English. Bickerton proposes that children are the authors of creole. Bickerton's hypothesis is called "language bioprogram." He claims that through the process of biological evolution, the capacity to produce a "highly-specified language, given only some (perhaps quite minimal) triggering in the form of communal language use" (296). Evolution has developed this capacity to the level of creole. Children who are the first creole generation are not taught creole by their parents, since their parents only speak a simplified form of pidgin they cannot teach them how to expand the language into creole. The children accomplish this expansion themselves, by relying on their own biological capacity to develop language into a creole under such dire circumstances. Since Beloved both represents Sethe's dead child (as well as the child who died during the Middle Passage) and perhaps Sethe's own youthful past, her language represents an Early Black English in the sense that it is an attempt of a new generation of young children to advance a lexical synthesis of past and present languages.

Beloved's use of language may be compared with the use of Hawaiian Pidgin English (HPE). As Derek Bickerton observes, speakers of HPE must work with "minimal vocabulary and narrow range of structural options" (14).

To illustrate his point, he quotes one HPE speaker who, like Beloved, must find "ingenious ways of replacing lexical items which they lack or are unsure of" (14). As a substitute for the word "library" this speaker uses the phrases, "that book anything borrow can place," and "That place where you can borrow any of the books" (14).

Likewise, Beloved's language is the result of a beginner's attempt to become familiar with and articulate in the English language. Like any other people for whom English is a second language, or creole, the slaves which Beloved represents must have had a hard time finding the words to express their ideas to make the new language meaningful. Beloved's use of the word "diamonds" to suggest both earrings and crystal; and her use of the word "fix" to suggest comb, heal, caress, and tie, is another. Perhaps her limited English vocabulary does not yet include the words "comb" or "caress" or "tie."

In contrast to the language used to represent Beloved's speech, another kind of language is used to represent Beloved in the "poetic chapters." As I discuss in Chapter 3, the poetic chapters, consist of monologues by Beloved, Sethe, and Denver, and a collective dialogue between all three characters (200–217). Stamp Paid recognizes these voices but finds them "undecipherable;" they are "unspeakable thoughts unspoken" (199). In these chapters, Beloved reveals more about her experience during the Middle Passage.

This revelation occurs in a language which is noticeably different in its grammatical structure from the language Beloved uses when she speaks. The language used outside Beloved's chapter is designed to reproduce the sound of Beloved's dialect; however, the language used inside the chapter calls attention to its structure as writing, not speech. It does not constitute the same kind of grammar, punctuation, and syntax used to suggest the colloquial sound of Beloved's dialect. Furthermore, the language inside the poetic chapter does not wield a sophisticated use of punctuation; and its grammar and syntax suggest a variety of English that is, in some ways, closer to standard English than the one Beloved uses outside the chapter.

A comparison between the language Beloved uses inside and outside the poetic chapters illustrates this point. The following example records Beloved's speech outside of the poetic chapter.

> Hot. Nothing to breathe down there and no room to move   in . . . Heaps. A lot of people is down there and no room to move in. (75)

The punctuation, grammar, and syntax are made to reflect the sound of colloquial speech. The period which separates "hot" and "nothing" does not reflect a division of standard syntax. Rather, it is used to show a long pause, which often accompanies the natural rhythms of speech, between the first utterance and the second. The same is true between the second and third sentences. The grammar produces the sound of colloquial speech when it drops the past tense markers and when the subject and the verb fail to agree.

Contrast this example to this excerpt from Beloved's poetic chapter:

> I AM BELOVED and she is mine. I see her take flowers away from leaves she puts them
> in a round basket the leaves are not for her she fills the basket she opens the grass
> I would help her but the clouds. . . . (210)

There are no consistent punctuation and capitalization, features which visibly register in writing the long or short pauses which order and characterize speech. In the first sentence, the first three words are capitalized, and the letter "I" is capitalized whenever it appears; but no other letters are capitalized. Only the spaces between what appear to be sentences give meaning to the syntax. Another failure to represent the sound of dialect occurs with the appearance of subject verb agreement and tense markers that match the time frame. In this regard, the grammar of Beloved's poetic chapter is closer to standard English and fails to reflect the grammar of her colloquial speech.

Is Beloved's grammar different from the language which is used by Sethe and Denver in the other poetic chapters? Oddly enough, Beloved's monologue is the only one in which the capitalization and punctuation are absent and the syntax is standard. The syntax, capitalization, and punctuation are used in the other poetic chapters to communicate the diction of colloquial speech with written clarity.[10]

Two examples from the other poetic chapters illustrate this point. Sethe's monologue displays a sophisticated use of punctuation and syntax. This grammar is not used in the service of producing standard English—rather, it is used to create the sound of long pauses and sudden interjections found in speech: "Maybe. Anyhow I took my babies to the corn, Halle or no. Jesus. When I heard that woman's rattle" (202). The incomplete sentences force the reader to pause and slow down, and to consider the possibility that Sethe too, is pausing, and slowing down when she thinks of these words. The dependent clause "When I heard . . . " is forced to serve as a sentence, an incomplete sentence. Such syntax renders her speech colloquial. At the same time, there is a certain kind of dexterity which is displayed in the writing of this sentence: her syntax is truncated because she is unwilling to fill in the details. The completion of the sentence would require her to relate the painful emotions she felt when she knew that time was running out and she had to make a decision about whether to run away from slavery with her children or run back to her husband who had not escaped. This kind of syntax frequents colloquial speech. However, it is unacceptable in standard English, which follows the dictate of standard linguistic law rather than the dictate of a state of mind.

A sentence from Denver's monologue reflects another side of this linguistic dexterity: it is an excellent example of how writing orders speech on the page, an aspect which is lacking in Beloved's monologue. In Denver's sentence, a long stream of speech is ordered by the use of punctuation: "And when she wondered about Ma'am's earrings—something I didn't know about—well, that just made the cheese more binding: my sister come to help me wait for my daddy" (208). Without the sophisticated use of punctuation displayed here, this stream of thought would not make sense on the page, even though it makes sense when it is spoken and ordered by intonation and rhythmic pauses. Punctuation, then, is used to make (written) sense of Denver's colloquial sound.

By contrast, Beloved's monologue does not attempt to replicate the sound of the spoken word; nor does it apply a sophisticated use of the conventions of writing to make sense in writing of the spoken word. For this reason, this particular monologue calls attention to its writing, as opposed to its sound. And for this reason, its peculiar grammar resembles basic writing, the writing produced by beginning writers. There are few records of unedited, written language of the slaves, and to my knowledge, there are even fewer significant studies of such language. Therefore, in order to support my hypothesis that Beloved's monologue resembles the basic writing produced by semi-literate slaves I draw from sparse and varied material. I compare the monologue to samples of letters written by slaves and collected (separately) by Jean Fagan Yellin and Robert Starobin; to Susan Willis's linguistic study of one slave's unedited writing; and to Mina Shaughnessy's study of basic writing, the writing produced by students who speak Black English and who are just beginning to learn how to write.

My comparison begins with an examination of the letters written by semi-literate slaves. Like the monologue, these letters do not display a sophisticated use of written language. Unlike many of the slave narratives, which were produced with the aid of abolitionists, these letters were not edited before they were sent. A striking example is found in the letters of Harriet Jacobs, who wrote *Incidents in the Life of a Slave Girl* under the pseudonym Linda Brent. Jacobs' narrative was edited by Maria Childs, who admits in her introduction to having made "such changes . . . mainly for purposes of condensation and orderly arrangement . . ." and notes that "the ideas and language are her own" (3). Quite likely, then, it is because of the editorial changes made by Childs that the grammar of the edited narrative and the unedited letters of Jacobs differ. The letters were collected by Jean Fagan Yellin who remarks in her "Note on This Edition" that in them Jacobs:

> capitalizes important words but omits capital letters at the beginning of sentences. Because in the early letters she also omits most punctuation, even final periods, in this edition spaces marking full stops have been inserted to aid the reader. (xxxiv)

Yellin highlights the differences between the unrevised and unedited letters of Jacobs and the edited language of "Linda Brent." In a fashion similar to Beloved's monologue, Jacobs' letters contain spaces (inserted by Yellin) in order to register written clarity when little or no punctuation exists. Jacobs' October 1853 letter to Amy Post is a case in point:

> I was more than glad to recieve (sic) your welcome letter for I must acknowldege (sic) that your long silence had troubled me much I should have written before this but we have had a little member . . . (236)

Jacobs uses the sophisticated vocabulary and syntax found in her narrative, but refrains from using a period to mark two sentences. One can only speculate why Jacobs omits the punctuation: perhaps she was in a hurry to finish writing and did not have the time to edit her work. However, it is clear why the punctuation is not absent from Jacobs' narrative. As I mention in Chapter 3, that the editors of slave narratives were especially concerned with the content and the form of the writing because it was subject to careful and critical scrutiny by often hostile audiences. Proponents of slavery could use any excuse, even flawed grammar, to argue that Blacks were incapable of reasoning and writing and should therefore remain slaves.[11]

Undoubtedly because they were not meant for publication, as were the slave narratives, the letters collected by Starobin were not edited; nor did he edit them when he published them. Some of the letters contain very little punctuation, or no punctuation at all. Like Yellin, Starobin also uses spaces to separate clauses where there is no punctuation in order to produce written clarity. Here is one example in the following excerpt from the letter of Anthony Chase written on August 8, 1827:

> I know that you will be astonished and surprised when you become acquainted with the unexspected (sic) course that I am now about to take, a step that I never had the most istant Idea of tàkeing (sic), but what can a man do who has his hands bound and his feet fettered He will certainly try to get them loosened by fair and Honorable means and if not so. . . . (120)

Chase's vocabulary is more sophisticated, his syntax is more complex, and his sentences contain more punctuation than the language used in Beloved's monologue. Still, the linguistic similarity is evident when one considers that Chase does not use standard punctuation to separate sentences. This is evident when he misuses commas and produces fused sentences. He uses a comma to indicate a full stop before he asks a question which is improperly marked as such: "But what can a man do who has his hands bound and his feet fettered?" The last sentence in this passage can only be inferred by the space which has been inserted by Starobin between the words "fettered" and "He."

The lack of punctuation and incomplete syntax not only links the monologue with the unedited letters produced by slaves, but also with the narrative produced by ex-slave Juan Francisco Manzano. Susan Willis, who analyzes his language, cites an example from the writing of this early nineteenth century Cuban writer, which concerns memories of his experience as a slave:

> I suffered for the slightest act of boyish mischief, shut up in a coal pit with not even a plank for a bed nor anything to wrap myself up in for more than twenty four hours I was extremely frightened and wanted to eat my jail as can still be seen needs in the brightest noontime light a strong candle for one to see anything inside it here after suffering . . . . (206)[12]

Despite the relatively sophisticated vocabulary, this passage also may be productively compared with Beloved's monologue. Several observations which Willis makes about this text shed light on the monologue. First, Manzano's grammar, including the lack and misuse of punctuation, the lack of coherent narration, and the proliferation of unconnected substantive phrases, reveal his unfamiliarity with the conventions of writing. In particular, what she calls "extreme parataxis," the absence of coordinating elements which connect grammatical units, renders in his narrative a "strong sense of immediacy" and "sensory data" but neglects causal relationships" (207).

Like Manzano's text, Beloved's narrative is marked by "extreme parataxis," which enhances the sense that the perspective is focused on the experience, the data of sense. As opposed to being self-consciously shaped for an audience, it is written for the self. Because its grammar lacks the connective apparatus which provides logical sequence and developed analysis of what happened, the monologue does not reveal the cause of what happened. This excerpt from Beloved's monologue is a typical example:

> We are not crouching now we are standing but my legs are like my dead man's eyes I cannot fall because there is no room to the men without skin are making loud noises I am not dead the bread is sea colored (211)

If, as Broad and Wyatt suggest, Beloved's monologue details the experiences on a slave ship, then it follows that this passage likely relates the experience of trying to stand after being cramped in close quarters next to dead people, listening to the White crew members yelling; finding that she has somehow managed to live through this experience; and finding that the bread she is given to eat is rotten. Each clause describes a perception, but, like Manzano's narrative, it is not causal. It fails to connect the events described and to provide the reasons the events occur. Instead, the narrative follows the progression of these assaults upon her senses and insists on placing the reader in her position, the position of being completely unaware of the reason why she is assaulted and what will happen to her next.

As Willis explains, a "perspectival" narrative details the experiences from the point of view of the narrator, whose "perspectives on the motives behind all the demands and actions which govern his life has been short circuited" (202). Both the peculiarity of the grammar and the perspective rendered by the grammar distinguish Manzano's text from North American slave narratives, precisely because of its disregard for conventions of (slave narrative) genre and of literacy (206). Beloved's narrative, by virtue of its grammar and its point of view, distinguishes itself from the genre of the slave narrative because it does not seek to place the perspective of the slave within the context of her surroundings. As mentioned before, Beloved's language does not seek to follow the conventions of order, sequence, and point of view peculiar to the genre of slave narratives.[13] According to Willis, these peculiar linguistic qualities render Manzano's narrative typical of Caribbean slave narratives, where the abolitionist's influence upon the narrative was not as strong as in the United States.

Beloved's monologue and the unedited letters of slaves have something in common with the writing of "Basic Writers," speakers of Black English who are just learning to write: they are both examples of the writer's failure to write for an audience. One of the best studies of the transition from basic to advanced writing made by Black college students was published by Mina Shaughnessy in 1977. At first glance, this study may appear irrelevant because of the fact that it does not analyze the writing produced by slaves and was published, in fact, one century after slavery was abolished. Yet, I find Shaughnessy's careful linguistic study helpful in developing a linguistic analysis of what occurs in the writing of Blacks produced within different historical or literary contexts. Namely, I argue that features of writing exhibited in Beloved's monologue and the slaves' letters may be compared to the language produced by the beginning writer who has not yet acquired the skills needed to translate speech into writing and to move within the conventions of linguistic organization and order expected of the standard written word. In short, Beloved's monologue has been written for the self and not for the other.

Mina Shaughnessy's landmark study contains her observations about why basic writers perceive—or fail to perceive—the relationships between punctuation and syntax. It provides a key to understanding the fragmentation and absence of punctuation in Beloved's monologue:

> . . . punctuation becomes a problem for the BW [basic writer] student, not because he has no competence with sentences at all but because the writing down of sentences introduces new competencies that he has not been taught, including not only a knowledge of the names and functions of the various marks but also an ability to manage the structures that writers depend upon to overcome the redundancy, fragmentation, and loose sequencing that are natural in speech. (This would include such structures as adverbial clauses and participial phrases in pre-subject positions, relative clauses, appositional constructions, and logical connectives like therefore or however). (27)

Here, Shaughnessy uses her analysis of the pattern of errors basic writers make to produce a composite sketch of the level of competencies which characterize such writers. Basic writers are unable to produce a variety of complex syntax which include the structures she mentions. Because they are unaware of the conventions of writing which make sense of language on the page, they often fail to use punctuation properly; syntax fragmentation is one result of such misuse. Beloved's monologue may be compared to Shaughnessy's description of basic writing in the sense that it lacks the variety of complex sentences Shaughnessy mentions. Instead, it is marked, for the most part, by simple independent clauses. Without the aid of punctuation to indicate the beginning and end of sentences, these clauses are fragmented. If it were not for the spaces which separate clusters of her words, it would be difficult for any reader to produce grammatical meaning from them.

In addition to the sense that is made within sentences, basic writing and the writing which characterizes Beloved's language mars the sense that is made between sentences. Shaughnessy observes that basic writers do not often make connections between sentences which organize paragraphs. As a result, their analysis fails to develop. More significantly for my analysis of Beloved's language is Shaughnessy's finding that the failure to make connections between groups of sentences stifles the depiction of memory and history:

> One senses in such passages that the writer is cut off from the thoughts that might be
> awakened in less restricting situations. The mind is not allowed to play upon the topic,
> to follow the implications that lie within statements, or to recover the history of the
> idea as it developed in the writer's mind. Instead, the writer moves abruptly from one
> point to the next, abandoning as he goes all possibility of elaboration. (228)

In stark contrast to the ease with which Denver and Sethe's monologues are
translated into writing (as evidenced by the sophisticated use of punctuation
and varied syntax both complex and simple for their language) Beloved's
monologue gives the impression that the struggle to relate what has happened
also takes place at the site of language. This impression is not merely conveyed
in the content of the clause "how can I say things that are pictures," but is also
evidenced in the form of the writing itself, which exhibits the features
Shaughnessy describes (210). In this passage from Beloved's monologue the logical connection between "she opens the grass" and "I would help her but the
clouds are in the way" is not apparent. This collapse in logic occurs frequently
and has the effect that Shaughnessy describes on its relation of memory.
Beloved's language fails to repeat history and this failure is largely symbolic of
her relationship to a history which, as the epilogue of the novel records, "is not
a story to pass on" (275). The fragments of language in the monologue insist
upon relating a story that fails to be clarified in writing.

The monologue, therefore, suggests a multitude of voices which distinguishes it from Beloved's speaking voice. This distinction is registered in the
degree to which it avoids the colloquial diction which marks Beloved's
voice. The voice of the monologue reflects a wider range of standard English
vocabulary—yet, it is semi-literate in the sense that the complexity of the writing does not reflect a high level of what Olson calls "metalinguistic awareness."[14]
If the other monologues of Sethe and Denver represent what is unspoken, then
Beloved's represents what has been unwritten: the experiences of the Middle
Passage from the perspective of the slave, and written for herself, rather than
for a hostile audience.

CONCLUSION

This study relies upon linguistic research to discover Toni Morrison's literary play on spoken Black English and her commitment to creating a written language which expresses the souls of Black folk. Such a language is ever evolving in literature, as writers continue to define and redefine the written form of a language for which there is no standard form. Each chapter explores Morrison's own contributions to the form of this language as she describes them in her essay "Unspeakable Things Unspoken" (23).

In this description, she expresses two goals. First, her goal is to write a language which produces the sound most often heard in spoken Black language. To this end, the writing must be "speakerly" and "colloquial." This goal entails the features most heavily associated with the traditional representation of Black dialect: the arrangement of grammar, syntax, and spelling to suggest its sound. Secondly, Morrison focuses on what cannot be explicitly related by "Black" features of language at all: the creation of a character's voice which is never heard: "shap[ing] a silence while breaking it." Morrison often uses standard English for this purpose; when she does, the language may be called Black—not because it has the looks conventionally associated with Black language (nonstandard grammar)—but because it serves the goal she has defined for achieving a language worthy of black culture.

The "Black Looks and Black Acts" are two sides of the same coin. The looks include the grammar, syntax, and spelling; and the acts include the ways in which Morrison uses language (regardless of its looks) in the service of representing race.

A paradox exists at the heart of *The Bluest Eye*. On the one hand, Morrison's language strives to approximate reality. Her de-emphasis of pronunciation and grammatical features of Black dialect accurately reflect a bi-dialectical reality observed by linguists. On the other hand, standard and Black dialects are infused with meaning and acquire symbolic value. Here creative literary style dictates a reduction of grammatical and orthographical features where you least expect it. Pecola's voice is a case in point. She speaks a variety of language closer to the standard when she is insane, and nonstandard English when she is sane.

Morrison analyzes how the words convey the atmosphere surrounding Black English through the structures of rhetoric and narrative in *The Bluest Eye*. The language is made to suggest the consciousness of the realm of orality—the conspiracy, intimacy, and silence which occur between and through the exchange of words within the universe of this novel. The language reveals the atmosphere of intimacy and conspiracy which forges the community that surrounds Pecola Breedlove and her family, and juxtaposes these unwritten ties that bind against the silence and alienation which surrounds and defines the discourse of the Breedloves. The construction of this atmosphere which excludes the Breedloves forges the construction of the Breedloves' silence without breaking it. In effect, Morrison creates a literary representation of what has only been spoken orally (or occurred only in the oral realm) within the African American culture, and represents what has been too traumatic to speak at all.

One example of the narrative structure which enables this silence to take shape occurs in Pecola's discourse with herself. Morrison turns up the volume of the unspeakable and unspoken by diminishing the preparatory material (writerly narrative), explanatory devices (quotation marks), and substitutional fabric (hidden dialogue) which accompany representations of unspoken thoughts elsewhere in this novel. When there markers are diminished, what becomes apparent is Pecoloa's fullest explicit expression of her thoughts, her voice. As a result, readers are given more immediate access to the recesses of this character's mind.

Beloved develops and expands the capacity of the narrative to shape the silence represented in the passage involving Pecola in the novel *Beloved*. I call such developments in narration and voice in Morrison's form of unspeakable and unspoken. In the narration of *Beloved*, unspoken thoughts of the characters are given fuller expression and greater control of the narrative than in *The Bluest Eye*. In fact, In *Beloved*, the unspoken thoughts of the characters noticeably determine the structure of the narrative. What Morrison has done is to present the realm of memory in written form. This written form includes the fuller recession of the omniscient narrator. There is much less contextualizing, editing, or connecting here than in *The Bluest Eye*. The little that is evident in *Beloved's* narrative recedes at the apex of the novel when Seethe, Beloved, and Denver—like Pecola—have a dialogue among themselves which is neither heard nor spoken.

However, there is a crucial difference between the "poetic" section of *Beloved* and the "madness" passage in *The Bluest Eye*. Pecola's dialogue is posited as the unfortunate result of her lack of verbal communication with the community; her dialogue is insular—no one in her community has access to it. In *Beloved*, the dialogue between Beloved and Sethe is the goal of the text. It represents a kind of freedom for Sethe who is finally able to tell her story (about slavery) and find an audience in Beloved. It represents a discursive site where a community of slaves and their memories reside. Beloved represents the memories of Sethe's past, memories that never have to be spoken aloud: it is recorded in the unspeakable unspoken language mentioned above at the apex of the novel. Beloved is like Pecola, but twenty years older. Her mad talk about the effects of race on her soul is no longer madness; she speaks for all Blacks (slaves) and not just herself, as does Pecola. In this sense, she speaks with a greater degree of power.

Finally, I focus on the grammar of Beloved's language. She represents varieties of English which may be placed on a continuum from unknown African languages to varieties of written and spoken English. Her language represents the history of the languages spoken by slaves during the passage from Africa to America and the passage from slavery to freedom.

The findings of this dissertation demonstrate the wealth of complexity in Toni Morrison's language and the need for increasingly sophisticated scholarship to closely examine all of the novels, specifically, and the literature of Black Americans, in general.

NOTES

Contents

1. The title of this chapter is inspired by the Word of God. In Hebrews, Chapter II, verse 1, it reads: "Now faith is the substance of things hoped for, the evidence of things unseen." Just as literary criticism lays bare the unseen, diligent study of—and faith in—the Word of God yields the evidence of His presence.
2. Daniel 10:6.

Introduction

1. The work of William Labov, J.L. Dillard, Robbins Burling, Ralph Fasold and Roger Shuy are some of the best known linguists who belong to this category.
2. According to linguist Geneva Smitherman, the Black English is used by "80 to 90 percent of American Blacks" (2).
3. There are no extensive records of Black English in the mass media prior to the nineteenth century (Smitherman, 8).
4. From unpublished manuscript in collection of Ohio Historical Society. Quoted in Brasch (48).
5. Thomas Nelson Page, Paul Lawrence Dunbar, and Joel Chandler Harris published dialect tales and poems during the Reconstruction.
6. George Frederickson gives the following examples of authors who wrote plantation romances during the 1820's and 1830's: George Tucker, William Gilmore Simms, James Kirke Paulding, John Pendleton Kennedy, and Nathaniel Beverley Tucker (102).
7. Nora Kelecsenyi's article publishes similar findings.
8. Holloway's *Moorings and Metaphors* tracks figures of culture and gender in Black women's literature.
9. The contributions of Trudier Harris, Karen Carmean, Karla Holloway, Jean Wyatt, and William Dahill-Baue lead the way towards filling these huge gaps in critical research. See Nellie McKay and Nancy Peterson for their extensive bibliographies on Morrison.

Chapter 1

1. I use the terms "Black dialect," and "Black English," interchangeably, as does the linguist Geneva Smitherman in her book *Talkin' and Testifyin'*.
2. In Chapter four, I discuss in greater detail the historiography of Black English.
3. The MacTeers live in a racially mixed neighborhood.
4. It differs from the italicized, internal monologue of the character Pauline (quoted above). Pauline's internal monologue is in quotation; Pecola's monologue is not.
5. Dubois argues that Blacks are ever conscious of themselves as seen through the eyes of the (racist) other.
6. For more on the trope of double consciousness in *The Bluest Eye* and in Morrison's other novels, see Denise Heinze.
7. William Dahill-Baue argues that Morrison "deliberately identifies Church with the Standard English of Whites, without representing him as a White character" (470). I agree with Dahil-Baue's observation that Morrison uses this character to rebel "against the notion that Black characters must exhibit stereotypical features of Blackness" (470). However, I would argue that Soaphead is a Black character who sees Pecola as the other (whites) sees her. To convey this idea, Standard English is the poetic device Morrison uses.

Chapter 2

1. The title of this chapter is inspired by the Word of God. In Hebrews, Chapter II, verse 1, it reads: "Now faith is the substance of things hoped for, the evidence of things unseen." Just as literary criticism lays bare the unseen, diligent study of—and faith in—the Word of God yields the evidence of His presence.
2. Since Black English does not have a standard written form, it can be viewed as a language which is, first and foremost, a language which resides primarily in the realm of the oral.
3. See Morrison's essay, "Unspeakable Things Unspoken: The Afro-American Presence in American Literature," from which this quote was taken, for more of her analysis of silence and voice, which are central themes in *The Bluest Eye*.
4. As Trudier Harris explains, Claudia's narration of experience (as a child) and maturity (as an adult) serves the function of opening gaps in narration which Morrison fills with other voices. Since Claudia as an adult cannot remember, and cannot tell the entire story, she must rely as a narrator upon her image of the women in the community telling stories. Harris observes that this image indicates the communal nature of storytelling in Claudia's community, and the fact that Claudia is among many griots who tell a story which belongs to her community (23).
5. Tannen hypothesizes that these linguistic signals "are correlated with such nonverbal factors as the use of broad facial expressions and gestures, as well as relatively close kinesic proximity and frequent touching during talk" (146).
6. Such demands upon the readers are similar to those made by novelists. Margaret Radar elaborates: "Novelists leave the relationships between statements implicit, letting readers do this work, but they must fulfill their contract with readers to take them beyond what they could imagine on their own . . . Novelists work for explicit images, vivid details, well

chosen words whose connotations deepen and enrich their denotations, setting in motion in the readers imaginative processes of the novelists' choice" (195).

7. My analysis here is influenced by Roland Barthes, who provides a structural analysis of a lover's discourse.

8. Trudier Harris observes that the existence of gossip in *The Bluest Eye* serves the function of allowing characters to "comment upon situations and provide exposition for crucial events in the novel" (23).

9. As well, the illicit sexual behavior discussed here foreshadows other such behavior in the text. For example, it hints at the gossip concerning Pecola's rape by her father (147–148), and the secret letter written by Pecola's neighbor, Soaphead Church, to God in which he confesses his preferences for little girls (139–143).

10. A similar linguistic event which more graphically depicts Pecola's exclusion is the gossip which occurs when she is raped (147–148). Here, a linguistic community denounces her. Claudia processes the fragmented talk heard in town about Pecola, similar to Mrs. MacTeer's gossip in the sense that the conversation we see on the page does not accurately represent what occurs in oral discourse.

11. See Roberta Rubenstein for a discussion of communities and pariahs in other novels written by Morrison. For example, in *Sula*, Sula "catalyzes the anxieties of those whose paths she crosses because . . . she lives out the amoral potentialities that most people repress" (132). In *Tar Baby*, Jadine is parentless, and "lacks a model of either positive mothering or "daughtering"; cultureless, she lacks a clear sense of how to achieve authenticity in either black or white worlds" (133).

12. Another example of language which falls in the category of partial representation occurs on pg. 24. Claudia describes a few of the words which always accompany Sundays: so full of "don'ts" and "set'cha self downs." Apparently, these words come from a pool of utterances and commandments which are issued to the young girls periodically.

13. The research comes from Tannen's essay, "The Oral/Literate Continuum in Discourse."

14. See Olson for a discussion on the role of formalized patterns of speech in the oral tradition (263).

15. I also discuss this event in the first chapter (5–6).

16. Theresa Towner notes that the title *The Bluest Eye* is a pun on the words, 'the bluest I', for Pecola is "pathetically isolated and lonely" (116).

17. I analyze the reason why Pecola imagines that her parents speak in Standard English in Chapter 1 (18).

18. Donald Gibson discusses the way in which the primer, and the structure of the novel reflect how our lives are "contained within the framework of the values of the dominant culture and subjected to those values" (162).

19. Susan Willis argues that Pecola becomes "the most horrifying example of the mental distortion produced by being "other" to white culture" (175).

20. Jane Keunz describes some of these effects. She argues that "interaction with mass culture for anyone not represented therein, and especially for African-Americans, frequently requires abdication of self or the ability to see oneself in the body of another" (422). The effects are seen when Pecola becomes mad and imagines herself split in two bodies.

21. See Chikwenye Ogunyemi and Michael Awkward for more discussion on Pecola's alienation from the community. Both writers argue that the community uses her as a scapegoat. Awkward develops this idea further when he argues that Pecola never learns the survival

techniques that the community uses to combat the debilitating effects of the White ideological values. She is the "perfect target of scorn for the blacks who are armed with this knowledge." As a result, Pecola becomes the "ritual object in their ceremonies designed to exhibit to the master their "rejection" of blackness" (73).

22. Barbara Christian makes a similar point.

23. See her essay, "City Limits, Village Values" (38–39).

24. I discuss this passage at length in chapter I (19).

25. Robin Laloff argues that italics are used as a device for indicating a kind of emotional response which occurs in oral discourse. It accomplishes this by "suggesting the modes by which oral discourse is made emphatic: rise in pitch and loudness" (247).

26. These terms are from the excerpt from "Unspeakable Things Unspoken, "which I quote on page two of this essay. I fully analyze the way in which Mrs. Breedlove's language is collo-quial and coded in the Chapter I (9).

27. Olson argues that writing has a bias towards autonomous language, and that the transition from "utterances to text . . . can be described as one of increasing explicitness, with language increasingly able to stand as an unambiguous or autonomous representation of meaning" (258). Margaret Radar presents another point of view. She argues that there is no essential character of the medium of writing (188).

28. I have analyzed the contents of Pecola's conversation in Chapter I (19). That analysis will not be repeated.

Chapter 3

1. See Gates and McKay, from which this information was gleaned, for a lengthier discussion of the slave's achievement.

2. I borrow the terms "I" and "Eye" from Robert Stepto in his fine and ground-braking analy-sis of slave narratives.

3. Douglass also wrote a third autobiography, entitled *Life and Times* (1893). The differences, with respect to the issues raised here, between *Life* and *My Bondage* are negligible.

4. We learn, for instance, that his mother was the only Black person in Tuckahoe, free or enslaved, who knew how to read (155). And Douglass pays tribute to her by ascribing his love for knowledge to her (156).

5. See Cassirer, p. 50–51; and Olney, p. 151.

6. Donald Gibson draws a different conclusion. He argues that in comparison to the opening passage of the *Narrative*, *Bondage and Freedom*'s emphasis on the family is intended to remind readers of the absence of family life and the "incompatibility of slavery and rea-sonably amiable familial relations" (161).

7. My observations about Brent and Douglass are not generalized conclusions about the entire narratives.

8. Helen Lock observes that Morrison, along with Paule Marshall (*Praise Song for the Widow*) and David Bradley (*The Chaneysville Incident*) have all engaged the collective unconscious in which the painful memories of slavery are buried. These writers accomplish this by challenging the conceptions of memory and time which "[fix] the past unchangeably [and] reinforces resistance to confrontation. . . ." (111).

9. In interviews with Marsha Darling and Gloria Naylor, Morrison describes how she obtained information about Margaret Garner. In the Darling interview, Morrison's comments on how she combined fact with fiction are consistent with the process she describes in "The Site of Memory" (249). The newspaper clipping on Margaret Garner can be found in *The Black Book*, a project on which she worked on while an editor at Random House, where it was published.

10. Indeed, Stepto's approach to the study of slave narratives involves examining the authenticating documents and the slave's narrative as a single body. Stepto examines the bodies in order to classify the degree of authorial control slaves had in their narratives.

11. Her authenticating document also has precedence in her own work. As Gibson notes in the *Bluest Eye*, Morrison manipulates the Dick and Jane primer in the introduction to suggest her subversion and appropriation of authenticating documents/master texts.

   Michael Awkward makes the same point. In addition, he concludes, "Morrison returns to an earlier practice—of the white voice introducing the black text—to demonstrate . . . her refusal to allow white standards to arbitrate the success or failure of the Afro-American experience" (63).

12. I hasten to add, that as Foley notes, the presence of the "documentary mode" is not limited to the African American tradition. See her essay for the location of its presence in White American and European literature.

13. As Valerie Smith observes, the omniscient narrator frequently appears in Morrison's first three works, *The Bluest Eye, Sula, and Song of Solomon*. She writes: "Occasionally her characters reminisce in their own voices in mid conversation. But more often than not an omniscient voice interrupts the narrative present to tell and interpret a character's personal history" (122).

14. I am indebted to a related point made by Stepto for this analysis. Stepto discusses the way in which Henry Northrup's presentation of self in his narrative is diminished. Northrup documents the events of experience unrelated to the story of his own self so that he may be seen to be objective (rather than subjective), so that he may gain status as an authority. As a result, Stepto argues, Northrup's "eye and I are not so much introspective as they are inquisitive. . . ." (237).

15. The impulse in African American letters to address one's story to a sympathetic other who is also the self is not unique to *Beloved*. David Walker addresses his abolitionist tract in his *Appeal to the Colored Citizens of the World* (1829). The character Janie in Zora Neale Hurston's *Their Eyes Were Watching God* tells her story to her best friend Phoeby and lets her know that she can speak for her because "mah tongue is in mah friend's mouf" (17). And James Baldwin addresses his letter about racism to "James" his nephew and his namesake in *The Fire Next Time*.

16. Denver first asks for help from Lady Jones, the Black school teacher when she realizes that her mother needs help (248). Rebecca Ferguson notes that "communication is the keyword of her course of action [and]. . . ."Morrison seems concerned to show that, as history can be outlived, so language can be enabling, not only as an instrument of power but because it is one of the crucial means by which we express and communicate" (123).

17. Marianne DeKoven provides an alternative view. She observes that the Clearing, which "has strong utopian resonance, with its anonymous provenance, its anti-instrumentality, its spaciousness, and its depth in the woods—the primeval nature of the American Eden" represents a "destroyed utopian possibility" (80–81). Her reading accounts for another aspect of complexity and paradox which cannot be ignored: Beloved is also an entity separate from Sethe. She tries to kill Sethe. This is why Denver seeks help, and why the community reconstitutes itself to save Sethe.

18. Diane Enns makes the same point in her essay (274). She also offers an alternative reading to that of critics, Carl Malmgreen among them, who argue that there is a danger of lapsed boundaries between the self and the other in these passages. Enns posits that the passages are "narrative[s] of desire for mutual recognition . . . [which] liberate language from the hierarchical and oppressive categories of subject and object" (274).

19. Jean Wyatt's analysis of language in *Beloved* helped me to understand the relationship between the physical and linguistic body in this text.

20. I would like to thank Fran Bartkowski for this suggestion about the difference between Beloved's and Pecola's voice.

21. Quoted in Denise Heinze's article, "Toni Morrison."

Chapter 4

1. Daniel 10:6.

2. In the passage where Beloved asks about "diamonds" Sethe also asks for clarification (58).

3. These hypotheses are also used to explain the origins of those languages existing in colonized nations called Creole, which is a mixture of the subordinate and dominant languages.

4. The earliest form of Dillard's theory appeared in the work of Melville J. Kerskovits, who, according to historiographer Glenn Gilbert: "proposed that the acculturation of Africans in the New World left considerable opportunities for the direct and indirect survival of African cultural traits, including language. . . ." (458). The development of Kerskovits's thought occurred in the 1920's and 1930's. William Stewart and Geneva Smitherman are also major proponents of this school of thought.

5. See Dillard, Chapter Five.

6. Dillard relies on Darwin Turner's *Africanisms in Gullah Dialect* for evidence of Africanisms in America.

7. Mufwene, Fasold, and Burling, are among the leading linguists who have established an intermediary position (See Schneider, p. 27, for summary).

8. See chapter three for more details on the representation of Beloved.

9. See Schneider for more discussion on this issue (27).

10. One notable exception is the very last part of the last chapter, the collective dialogue. Although capitol letters are used, there is no punctuation. However, the spacing is different from the spacing used in Beloved's chapter in which the syntax is separated by space. In this last chapter, each sentence occupies its own line.

11. For more discussion on this racist belief see Gates' Introduction to *"Race," Writing, And Difference."*

12. Susan Willis translates this passage from Spanish to English.

13. See James Olney for a description of the genre of the slave narrative.

14. David Olson defines metalinguistic awareness as the ability of the writer to reflect upon language as an object (261). Such awareness is related to literacy because it involves an awareness of orthography which marks syllables, words, sentences, and paragraphs.

BIBLIOGRAPHY

Abrams, M.H. *A Glossary of Literary Terms*. Fort Worth: Harcourt Brace College Publishers, 1998.

Andrews, William. *To Tell A Free Story*. Urbana: University of Illinois Press, 1986.

———. (ed) *Toni Morrison's Beloved: A Casebook*. Cambridge: Oxford University Press, 1999.

Awkward, Michael. *Inspiriting Influences*. New York: Columbia University Press, 1989.

Bakhtin, M.M. *The Dialogic Imagination*. Ed. Michael Holquist. Trans. Caryl Emerson And Michael Holquist. Austin: University of Texas Press, 1981.

Baldwin, James. *The Fire Next Time*. New York: Dell, 1962.

Barthes, Roland. *A Lover's Discourse*. Trans. Richard Howard. New York: Hill and Wang, 1978.

Baugh, John. *Black Street Speech*. Austin: University of Texas Press, 1983.

Beaulieu, Elizabeth. *The Toni Morrison Encyclopedia*. Westport, Connecticut: Greenwood Press, 2003.

Bibb, Henry. *Narrative of the Life and Adventures of Henry Bibb*. New York: Negro Universites Press, 1969.

Bickerton, Derek. *The Roots of Language*. Ann Arbor: Karoma Publishers, 1981.

Brasch, Walter. *Black English and the Mass Media*. Amherst: University of Massachusetts Press, 1981.

Broad, Robert. "Giving Blood to the Scraps: Haints, History, and Hosea in *Beloved*." *African American Review* 28 (1994): 189–195.

Brown, William Wells. "Narrative of the Life and Escape of Willaims Well Brown." *Clotel*. New Hampshire: Ayer Company, 1994.

Burling, Robbins. *English in Black and White*. New York: Holt, Rinehart and Winston, Inc., 1973.

Carby, Hazel. *Reconstructing Womanhood*. New York: Oxford University Press, 1987.

Carmean, Karen. *Toni Morrison's World of Fiction*. Troy: The Whitston Publishing Company, 1993.

Cassier, Ernst. *An Essay on Man*. New Haven: Yale University Press, 1944.

Christian, Barbara. "The Contemporary Fables of Toni Morrison." Gates, *Toni Morrison* 59–199.

Reyes-Conner, and Marc Cameron. *The Aesthetics of Toni Morrison: Speaking The Unspeakable*. Jackson: University of Mississippi Press, 2000.

Dahill-Baue, William. "Insignificant Monkeys: Preaching Black English in Faulkner's *The Sound and the Fury* and Morrison's *The Bluest Eye and Beloved.*" *Mississippi Quarterly* 49 (1996): 457–73.

Darling, Marsha. "In the Realm of Responsibility: A Conversation with Toni Morrison." Taylor-Guthrie 246–253.

Davis, Charles and Gates, Henry Louis, eds. *The Slave's Narrative.* Oxford University Press, 1985.

Dillard, J.L. *Black English.* New York: Random House, 1972.

Dekoven, Marianne. "Utopia Limited: Post-Sixties and Postmodern American Fiction." *Modern Fiction Studies* 41 (1995): 75–97.

Dorsey, Peter. "The Mimesis of Metaphor in Douglass' *My Bondage and My Freedom.*" PMLA 3 (1996): 435–450.

Douglass, Frederick. *Narrative of the Life of Frederick Douglass.* New York: Library of America College Editions, 1994.

——. *My Bondage and My Freedom.* 1855. New York: Library of America College Editions, 1994.

——. *Life and Times of Frederick Douglass.* 1893. New York: Library of America College Editions, 1994.

Dubois, W.E.B. *The Souls of Black Folk.* New York: Avon Books, 1965.

Eckard, Paula Gallant. *Maternal Body and Voice in Toni Morrison, Bobbi Mason, And Lee Smith.* Columbia: University of Missouri Press, 2002.

Enns, Diane. " 'We Flesh' Remembering the Body *Beloved.*" *Philosophy Today* (Fall 1995): 263–279.

Equiano, Olaudah. *The Interesting Narrative of the Life of Olaudah Equiano.* 1814, Ed. Henry Louis Gates. New York: New American Library, 1987.

Butler-Evans, Eliott. *Race, Gender, and Desire: Narrative Strategies in the Fiction of Toni Cade Bambara, Toni Morrison, and Alice Walker.* Philadelphia: Temple University Press, 1989.

Fasold, Ralph, and Shuy, Roger eds. *Teaching Standard English in the Inner City.* Washington D.C.: Center for Applied Linguistics, 1970.

—— and Wolfrom, Walt. "Some Linguistic Features of Negro Dialect." Fasold, *Teaching Standard,* 41–87.

Fisher, Dexter and Stepto, Robert, eds. *Afro-American Literature.* New York: The Modern Language Association of America, 1979.

Fredrickson, George. *The Black Image in The White Mind.* Connecticut: Wesleyan University Press, 1971.

Foley, Barbara. "History, Fiction, and the Ground Between: The Uses of the Documentary Mode in Black Literature." *PMLA* 95 (1980): 389–403.

Foreman, Gabrielle. "Earwitness: Female Abolitionism, Sexuality, and *Incidents In the Life of a Slave Girl.* Garfield 100–131.

Furguson, Rebecca. "History, Memory, and Language in Toni Morrison's *Beloved.*" *Feminist Criticism: Theory and Practice.* Ed. Susan Sellers. Toronto: University of Toronto Press. 109–129.

Gates, Henry Louis, ed. *"Race," Writing, and Difference.* Chicago: The University of Chicago Press.

—— and Nellie McKay, eds. *The Norton Anthology of African American Literature.* New York: Norton and Co. 1987.

—— and K.A. Appiah, eds. *Toni Morrison: Critical Perspectives*. Columbia University Press, 1971.

Gerard, Genette. "Time and Narrative in A La recherche du temps perdu" *Aspects of Narrative* ed. J. Hillis Miller. New York: Columbia University Press, 1970.

Gibson, Donald. "Jacobs, Douglass, and the Slavery Debate." Garfield 156–175.

——. "Text and Countertext in *The Bluest Eye*." Gates, *Toni Morrison* 159–175.

Gilbert, Glenn. "Historical Development of the Creole Origin Hypothesis of Black English: The Pivital Role of Melville J. Kerskovits." Mufwene 440–458.

Harris, Middleton, ed. *The Black Book*. New York: Random House, 1974.

Harris, Trudier. *Fiction and Folklore*: The Novels of Toni Morrison. Knoxville: The University of Tennessee Press, 1991.

Havelock, Eric. "The Oral-Literate Equation: A Formula for the Modern Mind." Ed. David Olson, *Literacy and Orality*, 28–47.

Heinze, Denise. *The Dilemma of Double Consciousness: Toni Morrison's Novels*. Athens: University of Georgia Press, 1993.

——. "Toni Morrison." *Dictionary of Literary Biography*. Ed. James Giles. Third ser. 143 v. Detroit: A Bruccoli Clark Laymon Book, 1994.

Henderson, Mae Gwendolyn. "Speaking in Tongues." Changing Our Own Words: Essays on Criticism, Theory, and Writing by Black Women. Wall 16–37.

——. "Toni Morrion's *Beloved*: Re-Membering the Body as Historical Text." *Comparative American Identities: Race, Sex and Nationality in the Modern Text*. Ed. Hortense Spillers.

Hooks, Bell. *Black Looks: Race and Representation*. New York: Routledge, 1992.

Holdon-Kirwan, Jennifer. "Looking Into the Self That is No Self: An Examination of Subjectivity in *Beloved*." *African American Review* 32 (1998): 415–426.

Holloway, Karla. "Beloved: A Spiritual." *Callaloo* 13 (1990): 516–525.

——. *Moorings and Metaphors*. New Brunswick: Rutgers University Press, 1992.

——. "The Language and Music of Survival." *New Dimensions of Spirituality*. By Karla Holloway and Stephanie Demetrakopoulos. New York: Greenwood Press, 1987. 73–49.

Holton, Sylvia. *Down Home and Uptown: The Representations of Black Speech in American Fiction*. Rutherford: Fairleigh Dickinson University Press, 1984.

Hurston, Zora Neale. "Characteristics of Negro Expression." *Negro: An Anthology*. Frederick Ungar, 1934.

——. *Their Eyes Were Watching God*. Urbana: University of Ilinois Press, 1978.

Jacobs, Harriet. *Incidents in the Life of a Slave Girl*. 1861. Ed. Yellin, Jean. Cambridge: Harvard University Press, 1987.

Johnson, Barbara. *A World of Difference*. Baltimore: The Johns Hopkins University Press, 1987.

Jones, Leroi. "Expressive Language." *Language, Comunication, and Rhetoric in Black America*. Ed. Arthur Smith. New York: Harper and Row, 1972, 323–329.

Joyner, Louisa. *The Essential Guide to Contemporary Literature*. New York: Vintage Living Trusts, 2003.

Kelecsenyi, Nora. "The Representative of Black English in Black Fiction After The 1940's." *Studies Anglica Posnaiensia* 28 (1994): 171–178.

Keunz, Jane. "*The Bluest Eye*: Notes on History, Community, and Black Female Subjectivity." *African American Review* 27 (1993): 421–431.

King, Lovalerie and Scott, Lynn. *James Baldwin and Toni Morrison: Comparative Critical and Theoretical Essays*. London: Palgrave Macmillan.

Khayati, Abdellatif. "Representation, Race, and the 'Language' of the Ineffable Toni Morrison's Narratives" *African American Review* 33 (1999):313–324.

Labov, William. *Language in the Inner City*. Philadelphia: University of Pennsylvania Press, 1972.

Lock, Helen, " 'Building up from Fragments,': The Oral Memory Process in Some Recent African American Written Narratives." *College Literature* 22(1995): 109–120.

Major, Clarence. *Dictionary of Afro-American Slang*. New York: International Publishers, 1970.

Malmgreen, Carl. "Mixed Genres and the Logic of Slavery in Toni Morrison's *Beloved*" *Critique: Studies in Contemporary Fiction* 36 (1995): 96–106.

McKay, Nellie and Earle, Kathryn, eds. *Approaches to Teaching the Novels of Toni Morrison*. New York: The Modern Langauge Association of America, 1997.

Mitchell-Kernan, Claudia. "Signifying, Loud-Talking, and Marking." *Rappin and Stylin Out*. Ed. Thomas Kochman. Urbana: University of Ilinois Press, 1997. 315–336.

Mori, Aoi. *Toni Morrison and Womanist Discourse*. New York: Peter Lang.

Morrison, Toni. *Beloved*. New York: Plume, 1987.

——. "City Limits, Village Values." *Literature and the Urban Experience*. Eds. Michael Jaye and Ann Watts. New Jersey: Rutgers University Press, 1972. 35–43.

——. *The Bluest Eye*. New York: Washington Square Press, 1970.

——. "The Site of Memory." *Inventing the Truth: The Art and Craft of Memoir*. Boston: Houghton Mifflin, 1987. 103–124.

——. "Unspeakable Things Unspoken." *Michigan Quarterly Review* 28 (1989): 1–34.

Mufwene, Salikoko, ed. *Africanisms in Afro-American Language Varieties*. Athens: The University of Georgia Press, 1993.

Naylor, Gloria. "A Conversation: Gloria Naylor and Toni Morrison's *The Bluest Eye*." Taylor-Guthrie 188–217.

Ogunyemi, Chikwenye. "Order and Disorder in Toni Morrison's *The Bluest Eye*." *Critique* 19 (1997): 112–120.

Olney, James. " 'I was Born': Slave Narratives, Their Status as Autobiography and As Literature." Davis 148–175.

Olson, David. "From Utterance to Text: The Bias of Language in Speech and Writing." *Harvard Educational Review* 47 (1997): 257–281.

—— and Torrance, Nancy eds. *Literacy and Orality*. Cambridge: Cambridge University Press, 1991.

——. "Literacy as Metalinguistics." *Literacy* 251–271.

Pagnattaro, Marisa. *In Defiance of the Law: From Ann Hutchinson to Toni Morrison*. New York: Peter Lang, 2001.

Peterson, Nancy J., ed. *Toni Morrison*. Special issue of *Modern Fiction Studies* 39 (1993): 461–859.

Radar, Margaret. "Context in Written Language: The Case of Imaginative Fiction." Tannen, *Spoken and Written Language*, 185–197.

Rubenstein, Roberta. "Pariahs and Community." Gates, *Toni Morrison* 126–159.

Schneider, Edgar. *American Earlier Black English*. Tuscaloosa: The University of Alabama Press, 1981.

Shaugnessy, Mina. *Errors and Expectations*. New York: Oxford University Press, 1977.

Smith, Valerie. *Self-Discovery and Authority in Afro-American Narrative*. Cambridge: Harvard University Press, 1987.

Smitherman, Geneva. *Talkin' and Testfyin*, Detroit: Wayne State University Press, 1977.

——. Black Talk: Words and Phrases from the Hood to the Amen Corner. Boston: Houghton Mifflin, 1994.

Spillers, Hortense, ed. *Comparative American Identities: Race, Sex, Nationality*. New York: Routledge, 1991.

Starobin, Robert, ed. *Blacks in Bondage: Letters of American Slaves*. New York: Markus Wiener Publishing, 1998.

Stave, Shirley, ed. *Toni Morrison and the Bible*. New York: Peter Lang.

Stepto, Robert. *From Behind the Veil*. 2nd ed. Urbana: University of Illinois Press, 1991.

Stewart, William. "Nonstandard Speech Patterns." *Baltimore Bulletin of Education* 43 (1966): 52–65.

Tannen, Deborah. *Conversational Style*. New Jersey: Ablex Publishing Corporation. 1984.

——. ed. *Spoken and Written Langauge*. New Jersey: Ablex Publishing Corporation, 1982.

——. "The Oral/Literate Continuum in Discourse." *Spoken and Written Langauge* 1–17.

Taylor-Guthrie, Danielle. *Conversations with Toni Morrison*. Jackson: Jackson Univesity Press of Missisippi, 1994.

Towner, Theresa. "Black Matters on the Dixie Limited; As I Lay Dying and the *Bluest Eye*" *Unflinching Gaze*. Eds. Carol Lokmerten., et al. Jackson: University Press of Mississippi, 1997. 115–128.

Turner, Darwin. *Africanisms in the Gullah Dialect*. New York: Arno Press, 1969.

Volosinov, V.N. *Marxism and the Philosophy of Langauge*. Trans. Ladislav Matejka I.R. Titunik. New York: Seminar Press, 1973.

Walker, David. *Appeal*. New York: Humanities Press, 1965.

Wall, Cheryl. Ed. *Changing Our Own Words*. New Brunswick: Rutgers University Press, 1989.

Willis, Susan. "Crushed Geraniums: Juan Francisco Manzano and the Language of Slavery." Davis 199–225.

——. "I Shop Therefore I am: Is there A Place for Afro American Culture in Commodity Culture?" Wall 173–195.

——. *Specifying*. Madison: The University of Wisconsin Press, 1987.

Wyatt, Jean. "Giving Body to the Word: The Maternal Symbolic in Toni Morrison's Beloved." *PMLA* 108 (1993): 474–488.

Yellin, Jean. "Text and Contexts of Harriet Jacobs.' Incidents in the Life of a Slave Girl Written by Herself." Davis 262–283.